EVERYBODY'S GYMNASTICS BOOK

EVERYBODY'S GYMNASTICS BOOK

BILL SANDS & MIKE CONKLIN

CHARLES SCRIBNER'S SONS · NEW YORK

Library of Congress Cataloging in Publication Data

Sands, Bill, 1953–
  Everybody's gymnastics book.

  Includes index.
  1. Gymnastics.   2. Gymnastics—United States.
I. Conklin, Mike.   II. Title.
GV461.S243   1984   796.4'1   84-1276
ISBN 0-684-18091-X

1 3 5 7 9 11 13 15 17 19   F/C   20 18 16 14 12 10 8 6 4 2

Printed in the United States of America.

This book is dedicated to the Koopmans: Richard, Judy, Amy, Melissa, Rick, and Suzanne. You have always been supportive of my virtues and tolerant of my mistakes. You have shown me generosity and taught me trust. I will carry this with me always. My sincerest thanks.
BILL SANDS

Thanks, W. C. The memory of you was with me while working on this book.
MIKE CONKLIN

CONTENTS

Contents

ACKNOWLEDGMENTS

We would like to thank the following people for their assistance and inspiration in the preparation of the material, participating in the photos, taking the photos, or generally putting up with our impatience: Diane Conklin, W. C. Conklin, John Zahorik, Sr., Basil Kane, Donna Cozzo, Dan Clemis, Dr. Lowell Weil, Sandy Sobotka, Nicole Trewitt, Katie McDivitt, Larry Kory, Greg Marsden, Lynne Lederer, Arthur Henning, Marie Roethlisberger, Paula Schaffner, Phoebe Mills, Gail Hamilton, Infinity Camera, Ika Lindholm, Tina Travlos, Lori Leafman, Carrie Swanson, Liza Smith, Amy Zeitz, Jennifer Cless, Jennifer Messineo, Sheri Oguss, Jennifer Jakopin, Ginny Kipka, Tammy Labuy, Mrs. Labuy, Mrs. Leafman, Mrs. Lederer, Kurt and Cora Buckowicz, Paula Wagener, Michelle Hagiguchi, Penn State, University of Nebraska, McDonald's, and the *Chicago Tribune*.

Bill Sands and Mike Conklin

INTRODUCTION

Gymnastics is an all-encompassing endeavor for participants and a beautiful and dramatic sporting event for spectators. In its modern form, it has gone through many changes and evolved into one of the most artistic of the competitive sports.

The early history of gymnastics does not give clear indications of the sport's evolution, because its early development in no way approaches the kind of gymnastics that we see today. The early contributors often did not have competition in mind and saw gymnastics as a simple means of elevating the fitness of the population.

Over the past thirty years the Olympic Games have drawn attention to modern gymnastics. This interest probably culminated through the back-to-back Olympic performances of Olga Korbut and Nadia Comaneche in 1972 and 1976, respectively. Great media interest, plus the pure artistry and talent of these young women, sparked an intense desire by the young people of many nations to enter training and create a higher level of the sport than had ever existed.

The modern form of gymnastics will probably be of most interest to you and that is where we will concentrate our efforts. We will describe the different events that men and women participate in now and discuss a new type of gymnastics called "Rhythmic Gymnastics" that will make its Olympic debut in 1984 in Los Angeles.

Judging competitive exercise and the rules that surround competition are complex. Judges must apply the rules right on the floor of competition. This is not true in other sports, where the rule book might be more extensive and explains explicitly how the game is to be conducted, and not simply how to evaluate it.

Each country has its own gymnastics administrative body, subordinate to the international governing body of gymnastics. International competition is sometimes handled differently from national competition; many rules only apply to one level. We will also discuss the many levels of organization this sport entails.

Gymnastics is a sport of thousands of individual skills that must be learned by the athlete, understood by the coach, and appreciated by the spectator. We will cover these skills in broad perspective to give the spectator an appreciation for their obvious aspects and subtle nuances. Due to the large number, only a few will be covered in specific detail. These difficult skills can appear deceptively simple: one of the goals of the gymnast is to make such skills look simple and effortless. This is unlike the case of the circus performer who must try to give the impression that the skills are very difficult and dangerous; his or her artistry depends upon the apparent risks.

One of the most consistent and loudly voiced frustrations of the spectator and young athlete alike concerns the difficulty of determining individual winners. After all, touchdowns, baskets and goals are easy to recognize. The winner in gymnastics is not always the person with flawless appearance, or the one who demonstrates the riskiest routine. Therefore, a look at how events are scored is of vital interest to everyone in gymnastics, since these scores determine the winner.

We will also discuss the kind of training necessary. Training in gymnastics is different from most other sports because of the large number of skills that need to be learned and the level of quality necessary to distinguish the champion.

For the reader interested in pursuing the sport personally or introducing it to a son or daughter, we will also provide suggestions on how to locate a good program that will suit the needs and desires of the young person.

Gymnastics is sometimes seen as a dangerous and risky sport because of all the flipping and turning and possibility of falls. We'll address this issue as well. The fact is that gymnastics is not as dangerous as many other sports and, if properly approached, can provide years of personal accomplishment.

The current U.S. gymnastics stars are many and very promising. These stars form the public relations arm of gymnastics, as young people try to emulate their accomplishments. Unlike sports that have had their publicity problems, gymnastics remains one of the few strongholds of American values.

1

A BRIEF HISTORY
OF GYMNASTICS

The history of the basics of gymnastics dates from antiquity. The modern form of competitive gymnastics, however, goes back only to the very end of the 1800s. Since gymnastics means many things to different people, cultures, and time periods, we'll take a rather broad view of the word in looking at its evolution.

Gymnastics has meant everything from physical education to medical therapeutics. It has also been equated with acrobatics, athletic dance, circus performances, tumbling, trampoline, stage acrobatics, and contortionism.

Some texts covering the sport's history include paintings on cave walls, where figures appear to somersault over a large animal. Whether this activity is an origin of gymnastics or not is not as important as the fact that these activities are natural. A look at most any playground in good weather will find young people cartwheeling and rolling as if it were as natural as walking. It would seem reasonable to assume that early man may have indeed been involved in gymnastics activities as a means of movement and fun.

Gymnastics activities are an outgrowth of play, enjoyment of movement, and man's constant exploration of new modes of living. The Chinese originated an acrobatic art form that has rivaled gymnastics for its beauty and daring. Records in China, Persia, and Egypt have described a form of gymnastics that included some of the basic skills that are considered fundamentals for gymnastic training today.

Modern forms of Western gymnastics are probably of Greek and Roman origin. The ancient Greeks built many complexes of buildings known as **gymnasia** for physical education training. The **palestra** was a room in the gymnasium used for wrestling. Floors were often covered with sand; mats were unheard of at that time.

One definition of gymnastics comes from the Greek word *gymnos,* which literally means "naked." The Greeks found that it was neither comfortable nor practical to exercise wearing the garb of the day. Thus the gymnasium became a place of naked or near-naked physical sporting events.

The gymnasia became important meeting places for Greeks. Young men would go there to train and take their education. Older citizens would gather for purposes of teaching and fellowship. The gymnasium was perhaps the predecessor of the town meeting hall, village school, or clubhouse.

The Greeks started the Olympic Games as a symbol of their ambition and respect for the physical and tactical prowess of individual citizens. These Olympic Games began in 776 B.C. with a single footrace of around 200 yards. The games continued for about 1,100 years. Boxing, wrestling, throwing, jumping, and weightlifting were added to the games and the event grew more steeped in Greek tradition.

Roman civilization overlapped and followed the Greek. The Romans conquered the Greeks and, because they were not innovators on the scale of the Greeks, copied the games and Greek physical culture. But the high ideals of the Greeks, who put physical education on a par with intellectual achievement, were not maintained by the Romans. Instead, the Romans saw physical exercise as a means to create a more fit and powerful soldier and army for conquest and battle.

The famous Greek physician Galen gave many valuable insights into Roman physical education and a different side of gymnastics called "medical gymnastics." Today, medical gymnastics are what we might call therapeutics. Galen's principal work, called the "Caracalla," was largely ignored during the entire Middle Ages and this provided one of the strange turns of history. His work emphasized the keep-fit exercises of gymnastics, gymnastics for the masses as a means to better health, and, above all, that gymnastics should be fun. When Galen's work was uncovered centuries later, it became one of the important documents in gymnastics and physical education.

The Olympic Games were finally abolished by the Roman Emperor Theodosius in 392 A.D. Physical education was no longer compulsory, and the gymnasia were closed. Following this period, and perhaps due to corruption and the resultant fall of the Roman Empire, the western world entered the Dark Ages.

This period of medieval times saw ascetiscm as the means to fulfillment. Bathing, exercise, and physical culture were looked upon as evil. Gymnastics was not practiced for years except by acrobatic troupes.

During the Middle Ages there were no significant developments in gymnastics. It was not until the eighteenth and nineteenth cenuries that gymnastics would be reborn. The first place for this renaissance was Germany, where two of the most influential people in the history of modern gymnastics made a mark on the development of the present-day form. The first was Johann Guts Muth. He read the work of Galen, as did many other educators of this period, and put Galen's ideas to work in his own book, *Gymnastics for Youth*. This book had a profound impact on gymnastics and the physical education of European children.

Frederick Jahn was born in 1778 and is considered by most to be the father of modern gymnastics. Jahn's concern as a patriot was in freeing Germany from Napoleon. He began teaching gymnastics to strengthen his country's youth and formed the first outdoor gymnasium in the Hasenheid park outside Berlin. This was the forerunner of the German Turnverein or gymnastics center that has spread about the world to bring gymnastics and community social functions to citizens.

Jahn invented many types of apparatus; his gymnastic center in Hasenheid was a maze of ladders, leather obstacles, ropes, and bars. It appears that he had few concrete plans for his gymnastics program, but he was undertaking a system of physical training never tried up to that point.

Jahn was imprisoned for German underground activities resisting Napoleonic dominance. The police closed his Turnvereins and kept them closed for twenty-two years. The ban on gymnastics forced these patriotic athletes to make their apparatus smaller and portable and to conduct their activities indoors to avoid detection. This development made the equipment more useful and contributed to the popularity of indoor gymnastics that German emigrants took to other countries.

An outgrowth of Jahn's Turnvereins was the British Amateur Gymnastic Association formed in 1888. It was not long after this that women took an interest and began working with the same equipment. Due to the strength needed to work on the apparatus, women had to develop equipment to meet their needs.

Women's participation in vigorous exercise was met with considerable resistance by the medical and educational community of the nineteenth century. In fact, women's gymnastics did not really receive adequate acceptance until as late as 1952, when the Soviets performed at the 1952 Olympic Games.

Another important contributor to the early development of gymnastics was a Swede named Pehr Henrik Ling (1776–1839), the father of Swedish gymnastics. Ling became the director of the Royal Central Institute of Gymnastics in Stockholm. He thought that physical education should build endurance, agility, and power. Further, aesthetics, military preparation, medical concerns, and recreation should be pursued through physical education. He created a program of fencing, vaulting, free exercises, and light apparatus work on booms, ladders, saddles, vaulting boxes, ropes, and other devices. Much of his gymnastics program, however, could be done without apparatus, and his program was developed according to the medical and physiological knowledge of the time.

Adolph Spiess was a German who gained the title of "Father of School Gymnastics." Spiess studied Jahn, but viewed gymnastics as an important part of the school curriculum, while Jahn saw gymnastics as a part of activities away from school. Spiess thought that physical fitness could be enhanced by stiff precision. Calisthenics in large groups with emphasis on marching drills to music were his stock in trade. Many German schools adopted his ideas.

Franz Nachtagall (1777–1847) was a Danish leader in physical education. He believed in broad applications for gymnastics, but the French Revolution and Napoleonic wars forced him to carry on his ideas to strengthen the military. He was the first to stress the use of safety matting in gymnastics.

Gerhard Vieth (1763–1836), another German, published an encyclopedia of exercises using side and long horses and a horizontal pole that was the forerunner of the horizontal and parallel bars. Vieth also emphasized the mental and moral values of physical activity in addition to physical benefits.

As a result of European emigration to the United States, this country saw many European ideas playing a major role in the development of American youth and our educational system. In 1825 the Round Hill School of Northampton, Massachusetts, appointed Dr. Charles Beck as director of a physical education program. Dr. Charles Fallen was appointed to begin a program of gymnastics at Harvard University at about the same time. Both were students of Jahn. These early programs flourished for a time but were eventually dropped because of the "drudgery of physical exercises." Yet these first physical education programs in the United States gave gymnastics a strong foothold in early educational thought.

New England and New York saw a large number of Turnvereins during the mid-1800s. By 1860 there were over 150 of them in this country. In 1865 the American Turners, an early social club devoted to physical fitness, organized the Normal College of the American Gymnastics Union, later affiliated with Indiana University. At the Chicago World's Fair of 1893, 4,000 Turners performed.

The American Sokol is another organization that has contributed to American gymnastics. The Sokol is a Czechoslovakian program that originated in 1862 in Prague under Dr. Miroslav Turs. In 1865 a Sokol was initiated in St. Louis, followed by one in Chicago in 1866, and one in New York in 1867. In the United States, the Sokol organization was as much a fraternal club for maintaining ties with the old country as a club devoted to physical fitness.

The YMCA was founded by George Williams in Britain in 1841. George Williams, a salesman, was instrumental in fostering the growth of gymnastics by adding equipment for the sport to his facilities.

From 1920 to about 1950, there was a sharp decline in the number of gymnastics enthusiasts. During this time fewer and fewer Sokols and Turnvereins offered instruction, and as they began closing their doors fewer became sponsors of gymnastics activities.

The decline seemed to occur for a variety of reasons. Students became disheartened with the regimented and boring calisthenics of another era and another continent. School administrators interpreted the philosophy of John Dewey to mean that free play was more important than regimentation and discipline. People were not faced with as much manual labor as before; the strength and fitness gymnastics required put it further out of reach for the masses, who were not physically capable of learning the skills quickly. The joy of success was delayed and this caused frustration. Physical educators began teaching less demanding skills and activities because of the smaller element of risk and hazard. (Some felt physical education should be aimed more at allowing the physically fit an opportunity for success.) Perhaps most important, the rise of team sports brought a corresponding decline in individual sports. More people could be accommodated by team sports at less cost and with less effort. The team sports promoted other activities, such as marching bands, cheerleaders, pep rallies, and publicity. This rise caused an increase in facilities for spectators and a decrease in facilities for participating in other sports. Team sports were fashionable; individual sports were neglected.

All these factors contributed to the decline of gymnastics activity during this period and the sport was kept alive only through the selfless efforts of a few strong and valiant people. Gymnastics may be coming upon a similar period at present as we enter a new era of gymnastics for young people. The next few years and the choices made by the gymnastics community will help determine the path as a sport.

SOME OLYMPIC HIGHLIGHTS

FOR MEN AND WOMEN

The rebirth of the Olympic Games in 1896 in Athens saw gymnasts competing from only five countries. Competition was held for the horizontal bar, rings, and vaulting. The German team, competing against the wishes of the German gymnastics governing body, took most of the titles.

The second Olympiad was held in Paris and French gymnasts dominated the field virtually unopposed. Although there were 136 gymnasts from six nations, the French took the top six places.

In the 1904 St. Louis Olympic Games there was considerably more competition from Americans. Although the Swiss and Austrian teams dominated the games, an American team composed largely of members of an immigrant gymnastics club in Philadelphia took first place.

The first truly international competition was held in Antwerp during the Belgian gymnastics festival. France won over Belgium. The event was noteworthy because only teams, and not individuals, were evaluated. The competition consisted of calisthenics, vaulting, horizontal bar, parallel bars, and the pommel horse.

Alberto Braglia won the Games in Athens in 1906 and won later in London and Stockholm as well. He was noted for his invention of a movement on the rings known as the "cross." He was later officially regarded as a professional and was not allowed to compete in the 1928 Olympics at the age of 45.

The 1920 Olympics saw gymnastics move closer to the modern artistic form. The calisthenics and track and field type events were removed from the gymnastics category. However, the development of gymnastics after 1920 was fraught with problems. The International Gymnastics Association sought to standardize the sport and initiated the all-around competition. In 1928, the Games were better attended with eleven nations participating in gymnastics. The ninth international tournament saw the first fatal fall as the Yugoslavian Anton Malej fell from the rings.

Only five nations could afford to send teams to Los Angeles for the Olympic Games in 1932. The United States did well. The inception of the World Championships, which replaced the "International Tournament," began in 1934 when the first World Championship was held in Budapest.

The 1936 Games were held in Berlin under a distorting cloud of international tensions and political propaganda. The Germans barely outdistanced the Swiss team. The format of compulsories and optionals set at these Games has been maintained. The program of six events for men was also instituted.

In the 1948 London games, the Finns won the gold. The Soviet Union made its debut in Olympic gymnastics in 1952 and dominated the field. The largest number of teams ever (29) competed that year in Helsinki. The Russians won the next gold in Melbourne but the Japanese were closing in. The United States began to make its mark in Melbourne by placing sixth as a team.

The 1960 Olympics in Rome saw Japan finally overtake the Soviets for the team gold, a medal they would not surrender until 1980. The World Championships were also dominated by Japan during this era until 1979 in Fort Worth when they were beaten by the Soviets.

Japan did not attend the 1980 Olympics but placed third in the Moscow World Championships.

Now a new power has made itself apparent in men's gymnastics: China. The team's first world appearance was in the 1979 World Championships, where it proved to be a most formidable force. In 1983 the Chinese men won the team competition at the Budapest World Championships.

The women's participation in Olympic and world gymnastics began in 1928. The International Gymnastics League and the Olympic Organizing Committee dared to offer a highly controversial team competition for women; individual competition wasn't considered. Five nations entered, but in 1932 in Los Angeles, events for women were not included at all.

The Hungarians in the 1934 World Championships held a women's competition; they were one of the few nations in favor of it. The 1934 competition included calisthenics, horizontal bar, parallel bars, and vaulting. There was also a curious addition to the women's competition: gymnastics with hand implements. This was the beginning of Rhythmic Gymnastics, which will be an Olympic sport for the first time in 1984 in Los Angeles.

In 1936 in Berlin, the women's competition continued. Uneven bars were used for the first time, but floor exercise was still in the future. However, the rest of the Olympic women's program was established in Berlin.

World War II did not have the same disastrous effect on the women's competition as it did on the men's. Although women received a great deal of attention for the first time, they were still not allowed to win medals in the 1948 games in London. In 1952 during the Olympics in Helsinki the Soviet Union women competed for the first time and they truly dominated.

The present Olympic format of floor exercise, vaulting, balance beam, and uneven bars, revised from the format established in 1936, was begun in Melbourne in 1956. The Soviets won every event—the team, the all-around, and even the first six places in vaulting. In 1960, they displayed nearly the same dominance with seventeen nations competing.

In 1964 a Czech named Vera Caslavska finally dethroned the Soviet Union's all-around dominance by bringing her team to close contention with the Soviets. In 1968 in Mexico City, Vera Caslavska won the all-around again and three gold medals. The Soviets barely held their first place team title.

In 1970, the World Championships in Yugoslavia brought new attention and popularity to women's gymnastics and inaugurated a new queen of gymnastics, Ludmilla Turischeva. In 1972 the duel between East Germany and the Soviet Union was highly publicized and, of course, everyone became aware of the Olga Korbut phenomenon of the Munich Games (Fig. 1). The Russians won the team title again, narrowly defeating the East Germans.

In 1976 the Montreal Games had a new star in Nadia Comaneche as she won the all-around and Romania took second place behind the Soviets. The 1978 World Championships were held in Strasbourg in France, where the Soviet Union won the team title again along with the all-around through Elena Mouhkina. The 1979 World Championships in Fort Worth saw the first upset of the Soviet women's team in many years when the Romanians won the team

Fig. 1 *Soviet gymnast Olga Korbut was the darling of the 1972 Olympics.*

gold despite an injured Comaneche. The Soviets were second. A new power made itself known as the Chinese women's team made a strong debut. The Soviets regained the team title in the 1980 Olympics and held it through the 1983 World Championships.

Important American contributions to the international competition at the World and Olympic levels began in 1970 with Cathy Rigby winning a silver medal on balance beam. In 1976 Peter Kormann of the United States won a bronze medal in floor exercise at the Montreal games. In 1978, three Americans with medals were Marcia Frederick winning gold on uneven bars, Kurt Thomas taking gold in floor exercise, and Kathy Johnson winning a bronze in floor exercise (Fig. 2).

In 1979 the World Championships were highlighted by the bronze medal won by the U.S. men in team competition. Kurt Thomas won more gold on the horizontal bar and Bart Conner became the World Champion on parallel bars. Christa Canary placed the highest of the women by taking a fifth place

Fig. 2 *While the United States has never dominated the international scene, American stars such as Kathy Johnson have kept the sport at a high profile in this country.*

in vaulting. That year also marked the debut of a new gymnast personality. Young Tracee Talavera performed at the American Cup with exceptional ability and showed the United States that the American women gymnasts had a new prodigy.

The United States did not participate in the 1980 Olympics but returned in 1981 for the World Championships where Tracee Talavera won a bronze medal on the balance beam and Julianne McNamara won the bronze medal on the uneven bars.

The U.S. teams have placed, usually between third and ninth, in the major international competitions. First national coach, Don Peters, is beginning a systematic national program for women. The men's program, under the direction of Mas Watanabe, a former Japanese gymnastics great, has also made big strides in international gymnastics.

China is the newest contender in international gymnastics. The Chinese male gymnasts are among the finest in the world. In the 1981 World Championships, for example, a Chinese competitor got a perfect 10 in horizontal bar, although he ultimately placed third because of lower preliminary scores. The Chinese women have already struck gold with a world champion in the uneven bars.

THE RENAISSANCE
OF INTEREST IN GYMNASTICS

Much of the rise in interest in gymnastics is due to the female stars of the sport.

The monumental growth we acknowledge today began around 1970, when Ludmilla Turischeva appeared on national television and the American gymnast Cathy Rigby made a major breakthrough by winning a medal for the balance beam at the 1970 World Championships. The media appeal of this California pixie brought increased attention to gymnastics. Before this time, the sport had gone largely unrecognized by the media; gymnastics owes a great deal to the television coverage of competitions and personalities during the 1970s.

In 1972 several phenomena increased public interest in gymnastics. Olga Korbut made such an impact that she was credited as the princess of gymnastics. She and many of her Soviet teammates made numerous U.S. tours that brought a lot of money back to their country and created much of the rage for gymnastics.

Interestingly, Korbut was a phenomenon that almost didn't happen. She was actually the alternate on the 1972 Soviet team. If not for an injury and a late substitution, Korbut, and her impact on gymnastics, might never have occurred.

In 1972 the coverage of the Olympic Games brought a new light to an emerging feminism. Gymnastics is one of the few sports that allows a significant number of women to be involved in a highly aggressive and competitive experience.

Later years saw Korbut's continued success at the 1974 World Championships and on many Soviet tours of the United States. However, before the 1976

Fig. 3 *Rumania's Nadia Comaneche was the next to pick up the Olympic flame after Olga Korbut.*

Olympic Games a new star emerged to capture the hearts and interest of Americans and the world. She was Nadia Comaneche, from a highly specialized training school in Romania (Fig. 3). Due to her early triumphs at a very young age, she was considered an absolute phenomenon in the sport. She became European champion at the tender age of thirteen.

Comaneche's great impact on the sport was created by the level of difficulty and risk she displayed in her exercise, her technical excellence, and her seeming inability to make a mistake. Pound for pound, many experts believe that Comaneche was the greatest athlete of the decade.

The 1976 Olympics were touted as the duel between Korbut and Comaneche, but the duel never materialized because Comaneche was nearly unbeatable. She received scores of perfect 10's from judges who began scoring other gymnasts too high and had nowhere left to go when her routines came up. Almost everyone agreed that there were flaws in her routines, but the judges had to award perfection to keep the scores relative for each competitor. Since Comaneche's work was so much better than most of the others, she received scores that distinguished her excellence from the performances of the other gymnasts. Her youth and her extraordinary performances set gymnastics on its ear. No one involved with the sport was accustomed to seeing such high-level skills demonstrated so flawlessly on every event.

Interestingly, through the politics of international gymnastics, the sport could have lost the Comaneche phenomenon. In gymnastics, the order of competition in each event is very important for the team score. The traditional team lineup uses the weakest athlete first and moves successively through the team, ending with the finest athlete on that particular event. The scores "build" in a corresponding way.

The realty is that if the athlete does not go up last on the event, it is very unlikely that he or she will receive the highest score. This is because the earlier performers become the standard against which the remaining competitors are judged. In other words, if you go up early in the lineup you can forget about winning because the tradition of building scores through the competitive order will not allow the early athletes to get scores as high as the later athletes, no matter how good the performance might have been.

In the 1976 Montreal Olympics the Soviets chose to split the last competitive spots between their two top all-arounders, Nelli Kim and Ludmilla Turischeva. They divided the eight opportunities to go up last between the two gymnasts. The Romanians elected to have Nadia go up last on every event. Nelli Kim proved to be the greatest Soviet threat for the all-around competition but, unfortunately, the alternation with Turischeva lowered the impact of Kim's scores. The flavor of the competition and the building of the scores could have been changed if the Soviets had planned differently.

In 1976, Peter Kormann won the first Olympic medal in men's gymnastics the United States had earned in decades. His bronze medal was a major breakthrough for gymnastics in this country. Although the media did not play it up as much as the women's program, it did establish the United States men's program as a potential contender for medals in world-level meets.

After the 1976 Olympics, the Romanians took their turn at exhibition tours of the United States. Nadia Comaneche, who was perhaps not as personable as Olga Korbut, brought new standards to women's gymnastics—and youth, risk, and a degree of stoicism.

Comaneche, a highly trained thoroughbred of an athlete, looked upon gymnastics more as an opportunity to excel than an opportunity to perform. Very interested in winning, she displayed the quiet and thorough intensity usually attributed to adult professionals of other sports. The public had some difficulty coming to grips with her intensity. After all, Korbut had cried when she failed on her bar routines in the 1972 Olympics and appeared to wear her emotions on her shirt-sleeve. Comaneche was machine-like in her performance. The entire Romanian team's wins were due to a seeming inability to make errors. Thorough training for consistency at the expense of artistry has brought gymnastics from an art form to an exercise in competitive acrobatics.

It takes considerable experience and maturity to display the type of emotion that goes into a truly artistic performance. The Romanians seemed to be more interested in a consistent performance so that the rules of gymnastics would not allow the judges to take deductions, as errors are easy to spot. This lack of artistry is risky (because there is less chance to impress the judges) in an international arena and the trend initiated by the Romanian team has, indeed, altered the course of gymnastics.

Most of the public understands sports on only two levels—winning versus losing, and consistency of performance. The older, more artistic approach to gymnastics is much more difficult for the spectator to understand. The Romanians provided the public with real beauty, but it is the beauty of fine engineering rather than that of the more esoteric forms of art such as dance, ability to emote, and ability to communicate a message. The public can appreciate a performance that is completed without errors but, frankly, is not as adept at understanding the artistic qualities of dance and the performance of gymnastics.

This new and more technical approach to gymnastics was increasingly sought by many young girls with dreams of the gymnastics stardom. There were not enough female coaches and good choreographers to go around. Many young male gymnasts moved into the women's side of the sport and took up the slack with coaching. Their approach emphasized winning and technique because the technical aspect of men's gymnastics is more dominant than the artistic aspect. For the male coaches the technical approach was the easiest way to teach young gymnasts. The current approach to the sport is aggressiveness to achieve wins.

Two young male gymnasts from the 1976 Olympic Team, Bart Conner and Kurt Thomas, began to duel for dominance of men's gymnastics in America. Thomas' phenomenal rise began when he placed in the top ten in the World Championships in Strasbourg in 1978 and won a gold medal in floor exercise. Thomas, a member of the Indiana State University team, and Conner, from the University of Oklahoma, exchanged victories, created gossip, and aroused interest in men's gymnastics. Young, small, clean-cut, and above all, good gymnasts, they were clearly a new image in American sports.

The increase of interest in gymnastics also brought an increase in private sector training of these young people. As the needs for high-level expertise could not be met by public schools, private gymnastics schools for both sexes at all levels and ages were opened. These gym clubs are run by people of varying qualifications and interests in competition. They have their own organization under the United States Gymnastics Federation (USGF), the United States Association of Independent Gymnastics Clubs (USAIGC). This organization sprang from a need for private clubs to enhance their business position and their ability to train young athletes.

The movement of the sport out of the public schools and into the private sector has been both a blessing and a problem. The private area of gymnastics is truly doing the much-needed job of educating the pre-adolescent gymnast, a task that the public schools cannot hope to do. Unfortunately, the private sector of gymnastics also suffers from the whims of the economy and the business sense of each individual owner and director. Even though a club may be very productive gymnastically, it may still fail monetarily. Small businesses are always in jeopardy and gymnastics clubs are no exception. As we move into the 80s, the effects of the economy will be felt and perhaps require a new movement.

Television has been a great asset to gymnastics in this country. According to the USGF, gymnastics is the most popular television sporting event after football. Most revenues supporting the USGF and its programs come from contracts to televise competitions. The future of gymnastics will be largely determined by television (Fig. 4).

The demand for "name" athletes on television to attract advertisers and viewers puts some new pressure on the training of young athletes. It also subjects national programs to income variations beyond the control of coaches and trainer.

A "Pro Tour" lasted for nearly two complete tours and provided some first-time professional competition for young gymnasts, notably Kurt Thomas. After public interest declined, the tour was ended, but not without opening some new avenues for the gymnastics experience.

Finally, there has been some important corporate interest in supporting the sport and the upcoming 1984 Olympics in Los Angeles. Both the McDonalds Corporation and Nissan support the U.S. Gymnastics Federation by funding and sponsoring activities. The need for support from the private and corporate sectors of American society is increasing.

In turn, demands placed upon gymnastics to reciprocate for this support may make the sport take a new and interesting turn in the next few years. As the difference between gold and silver is often green, these supporters may have a tremendous impact on United States international performance, and on the training and goals of the young gymnast.

Fig. 4   *Cathy Rigby keeps gymnastics popular in this country by applying her skills to show business.*

2

A PANORAMA
OF GYMNASTICS

Gymnastics is an esoteric and unusual sport.

The typical spectator, and even the involved parent and gymnast, often does not understand the panorama of gymnastics across the United States and the world. The reasons for confusion are many.

First, the rules are difficult to understand. Hardly anyone can predict the winner in competitions unless he or she knows everything behind the scenes. Second, there are a number of organizations and national and state champions. No one can be really sure who is the best and, in fact, who is the true state or national champion. Rules vary from organization to organization and change from year to year, sometimes from month to month. A 9.5 at one competition might earn only an 8.5 at another level. For the typical lay person unraveling all of these facts is frustrating. Let's begin taking a general look at how gymnastics works. Since competition functions in layers, or levels, we'll begin with the outermost and simplest layers before getting to the inner and more complex ones.

The international level includes the Olympic Games, the World Championships, and the World Cup, European, Pacific, and Pan American Championships. It also includes dual and invitational meets between two or more countries. This layer has the most media coverage, the fewest participants, and is usually the goal of most of those competing in the inner levels.

This layer is governed by the Federation of International Gymnastics. The FIG, an international organization, is responsible for developing the rules for competition, judging, and compulsory exercises that are used in the gymnastics competitions between nations. The FIG is composed of 78 nations. All these nations are responsible for following the FIG rules in competition among nations.

Most countries simply apply these rules or variations of them to their own domestic competitions. The United States has its own committees to interpret and adapt FIG rules to meet the needs of the American system. But when Americans compete with another nation, FIG rules are followed without change. This ensures consistency from one competition to another. Standardization is important in the turbulent and volatile world of international sport.

The FIG has a men's and a women's program. It elects officers and maintains other committees on technical matters, compulsories, and executive decisions. Committee membership is highly prized; each country seeks representation to ensure that its needs and aspirations are looked after. The value of elements or skills in gymnastics, sites for important competitions, and access to important people are largely controlled by these committees. It is vitally important that the reader understand that the international arena for gymnastics is as much a political arena as a performance arena, often more so.

It may not seem immediately apparent why committee membership and the FIG's role are so important to each gymnast and country. The selection of competition sites is important to the outcome of the competition. The home-court advantage definitely exists in gymnastics. The site also sometimes determines who will participate and who will not. The poorer nations may avoid going to important competitions that are halfway around the world. Most European nations that control the FIG due to a preponderance of membership in the various committees work hard to maintain the home advantage and the lesser cost of transporting their entire delegation to another part of the world. Therefore, there has been only one World Championship in gymnastics held in the United States.

In women's gymnastics, some points are awarded for originality in skills. The confirmation of the development of a new skill by performing it for the first time is very impressive in gymnastics. Historically, the skill has been named for the first person to perform it. The women's side of the sport has tried to systematize this by requiring each country to submit its "original" skills for evaluation and crediting. The technical committee of the FIG decides which skills are given "originality credit." The first person to perform a new skill in international competition is awarded 0.2 points (out of a possible 10 points for the routine) as an originality credit. Then as other people use the skill they get .1 points. What does this mean? The countries that get the most number of original skills approved could have a significant advantage in evaluation, since they can get several extra tenths in score. And the winner in gymnastics is usually decided by a rather small margin of points. The committee that rules on the originality of skills is made up mostly of Communist bloc countries and therefore the skills of those nations are more likely to get approved for originality credit. Though it is not always blatant, those countries who are in contention to dethrone the reigning powers are the most likely to suffer from the small edicts of the technical committee—an example of gymnastics serving as a political arena.

The FIG designs and implements a new compulsory set of exercises or routines every four years and determines the specifications for all the necessary apparatus. Athletes expecting to compete in international competition must perform these compulsories. There are some competitions, such as the World University Games, that perform optional exercises only. The Pan-American Games use their own compulsories.

These compulsories are called Olympic compulsories because they are usually determined right after the Olympic Games and are performed at the next Olympic Games. There has been some movement to change the format of FIG competitions to remove compulsories, but this has so far been defeated, largely because the less developed nations find them necessary to continue progress in their lower levels of performance quality and technique (see the section on compulsory exercise in Chapter 4).

Specifications for equipment begin with the FIG and are handed down to each national governing body and manufacturer of gymnastics equipment. This ensures that apparatus is constructed and designed in the same way across the world. This ruling has also ensured the continued dominance of a European equipment company which has traditionally provided most of the equipment for the world championships and Olympic Games.

Interestingly, American equipment companies have been largely responsible for innovations in equipment that have largely been adopted by the FIG and other equipment companies across the world. Examples of this innovation are fiberglass uneven bar rails, parallel bars, and rings, and a cushioned "spring floor" that provides considerably more safety and comfort in floor exercise.

The FIG is also responsible for maintaining its own system of judges. The judges are selected from many nations through testing and evaluation and are specially recognized as being eligible for judging international competitions.

The U.S. National and Elite levels in the United States are the next layer below the international level. These levels are occupied by athletes eligible for international competition and national championships. The U.S. nationals are sponsored by a variety of associations, such as the AAU (Amateur Athletic Union), NCAA (National Collegiate Athletic Association), USGF (United States Gymnastics Federation), USAIGC (United States Association of Independent Gymnastics Clubs), USECA (United States Elite Coaches' Association), and other members of the alphabet soup club. They each crown a "National Champion." Who is really the national champion? Let's put these organizations in perspective.

All of these groups are members of the U.S. Gymnastics Federation (USGF), our national governing body for gymnastics for men and women, including the new field of rhythmic gymnastics. The USGF has the sole right and responsibility to crown a national champion and select the U.S. teams for Olympic and World championships and others for lesser international contests. Other nations have similar governing bodies. Great Britain has the British Amateur Gymnastics Association; Denmark has Dansk Gymnastik Forbund. Each of these governing bodies is responsible for its national championships and for selecting its international teams and athletes. We can illustrate some other responsibilities by using the U.S. Gymnastics Federation as an example.

The USGF is officially recognized by the FIG as the voice of gymnastics in this country. The USGF is also recognized by the U.S. government as its official organization for gymnastics. It's responsible for international contests held in the United States and competitions abroad to which we send athletes. The USGF is also responsible for general business affairs of the sport.

The USGF in turn is composed of many other organizations. Some of these are the National Collegiate Athletic Association (NCAA), American Turners, American Alliance for Health, Physical Education, and Recreation, National Association of High School Gymnastics Coaches, National Federation of State High School Associations, National Junior College Athletic Association, National Gymnastics Judges Association, YMCA, American Sokol Organization, AAU, National Association of Intercollegiate Athletes, U.S. Association of Independent Gymnastics Clubs, and the U.S. Elite Coaches Association. Each of these organizations conducts its own events or contributes to competitions such as judging associations. The groups may have special permission to use their own national championships as qualifying meets to get their athletes to the USGF national championships, the Championships of the USA. Within each of these organizations there is a system of competition, administration, rules interpretation and adaptation, and goals.

The USGF conducts programs similar to those of its member organizations and to those of other nations around the world. There is an age group or developmental program to help bring athletes along from the beginning of training to compete for the United States or represent some major member institution in high-level competition. USGF age group programs are designed for men and women and are conducted in every state. Each state, in turn, has its own state championships, usually the preliminaries to regional and national championships.

The top echelon of the USGF program is the Elite level. The Elite events determine the selection of the U.S. national teams. It is from this level that the United States get its Olympic and world championship teams. In other words, athletes must set their sights on the Elite level before they can begin to have Olympic and world aspirations (Fig. 5).

The Elite program is divided into junior and senior programs. The seniors

Chris Riegel

Fig. 5   **SOME ELITE U.S. GYMNASTS,
(PAST AND PRESENT)**

Bart Conner

Scott Johnson

Gina Stallone

Jim Mikus

Tim Daggett

Tracee Talavera

Julianne McNamara

Dianne Durham

are those athletes, ages fifteen and over, who are eligible for the Olympic Games and World Championships. If the Olympic Games are in July in 1984, an athlete who is fifteen years old in 1984 would be eligible. This would have been a problem in 1976 when the now-famous Nadia Comaneche was not yet fifteen. The raised age requirement has somewhat divided the world of the Elite level gymnast. There are some very talented children younger than fifteen who cannot be on the Olympic and World Championship teams even if they are good enough. (Tracee Talavera was forced to sit out the 1979 World Championships due to her youth.) The junior Elite level, composed of these young children, has international competitions and many national competitions. Junior athletes usually do not perform the Olympic compulsory until they are fourteen, if female, and perform a slightly different compulsory if they are male. These junior athletes are the future of the senior level USGF programs and are highly respected and looked after. The gymnasts must also compete in the all-around. That means they must compete on all six events for men and four for women.

The junior Elite gymnasts are selected in competitions within their own age groups (which differ from one sanctioning body to another) and by the national coach and his staff. The junior program is designed to assist talented young athletes in developing their skills to their peak as they reach the senior level. The junior Elite program for men has proven to be especially productive and is a source of pride for the men's national program director. The women's junior program is much newer and its productivity is therefore more difficult to judge.

The Elite program and the title of "Elite" gymnast are sought after and prized by the young athlete. The road to becoming an Elite gymnast is long and hard. Most of these athletes start in the age group program and remain there for a few years before working their way up through the qualification system.

The more plaudits that the young gymnast earns at the Class I nationals, the more likely it is that the gymnast will have the requisite skills and abilities for the Elite program. The serious aspiring Elite gymnast begins by doing well at the Class I nationals. Then, he or she begins working the Elite compulsories and attending local clinics and symposia for developing skills and routines. Next comes a regional competition where he or she must achieve a certain score before moving to the next level, a national qualifying meet, or national meet, depending upon whether the gymnast is male or female. Senior men can also use college nationals to qualify for Elite national championships or the Championships of the USA.

After getting past the regional competition, the gymnast is considered an Elite gymnast. To make the national team, the athlete must qualify for the United States nationals, where the top twenty-one or so finishers are named to the final squad.

The junior and senior national teams for men and women include about 85 gymnasts. These young athletes are the ones in whom this country places its hopes for international competition.

The latest USGF records show about 37,000 registered male and female athletes in the USGF program. There are 3,000 and 4,000 males and approximately 33,000 registered and competitive female gymnasts. The USGF boasts a total membership of about 110,000 athletes, coaches, and judges, all of whom are actively involved in gymnastics. Others participate in schools, YMCAs, Sokols, Turners, and private clubs. The Elite level consists of fewer than 300 gymnasts, men and women.

The level just below Elite is the Class I, or Advanced level. This level conducts local and national championships with its own special compulsory exercises. It is where most of the future national and international stars of the U.S. start. Competition consists of the all-around program. Athletes must perform on all events; the gymnast cannot specialize on one or two events.

The next level is the Class II or Intermediate level. This consists of athletes who are not as skilled as the Class I athletes. In general, they are younger and less experienced, but this does not always hold true. The Class II level has competition from the local to the regional level. Class II has its own set of compulsories and sometimes different qualifying scores. Competition is in the all-around format.

The Class III level is for beginners even though the compulsories might seem quite advanced for a real novice. The Class III's also perform in the all-around format and have their own compulsories. The qualifying scores might be different from the other levels. Competition is offered as far as a state championship.

The next levels exist in different forms. The women's program has a Class IV compulsory, but some of the men's Class IV states do not. Some male programs have developed their own local compulsories for young men below the Class III level. Class IV is largely recreational, but has local and state competition.

Each level in the USGF age group and Elite programs has increased numbers of participants as the level of performance decreases. Each level in the women's program has its own judges. In the men's program, all judges participate in similar evaluation but are usually chosen for jobs by reputation and experience.

Administration below the actual national office is done by volunteers. The volunteer state and regional chairmen, technical directors, etc., are the backbone of the USGF and the gymnastics administration in the United States.

Another layer consists of organizations in each country that do not have the ability to compete internationally, but may allow the athlete to qualify to a higher USGF level and thereby enter international competition. Other organizations that compete in gymnastics have their own variations on the age group theme or offer competition to a special narrow group of athletes. High schools, for example, offer competition that usually culminates in a state championship.

The high schools allow specialists, or those who compete on fewer events than the all-around format. The specialist appears only in the United States and has been a major part of high school and collegiate gymnastics for many years. In fact, in the early development of gymnastics in the public schools the specialists were usually doing the best work. The specialist is still allowed in the NCAA format. Although specialists are not currently allowed in the international format, they have been in the past, depending upon when and where the meets were held.

The specialist helps make gymnastics more universal in its appeal. Not all gymnasts can be competent all-around athletes, and those that are exceptional at one or two events can find considerable enjoyment and achievement by training their favorite events to high levels. The Turners and Sokols, both featuring specialized gymnasts, have local and national meets along with other activities that are inherent to their traditions.

The innermost level is that of recreational and instructional gymnastics, where gymnasts are in the earliest stages of training or are participating in gymnastics as a part of physical education. This layer is by far the largest and includes people from all around the world.

Let's take a brief look at those programs not intimately related to the USGF programs and not necessarily devoted to developing athletes for international competition. These programs are equally important to gymnastics, but do not receive the media attention that would make the lay person aware of their purposes and goals.

One of these organizations is the YMCA, which has offered competition for many years in gymnastics and has provided some of the members of national teams and international performers. Right now, YMCA programs are not as active at the highest levels, but they still offer many fine programs and should receive much of the credit for keeping the sport alive and moving forward through hard times.

The Turners and Sokols are still alive and well in the United States. One of the authors, Bill Sands, received his early training with the Swiss Turners of Monroe, Wisconsin. The Turners and Sokols are still very important to the early development of young gymnasts, particularly in cities and neighborhoods with a strong Slavic and European ethnic background. For example, Jim

Hartung and Phil Cahoy, two fantastic gymnasts from the University of Nebraska, both members of the 1971 World Championships team, are still members of the Omaha Sokol and take part in the traditional Sokol national meet. Tim Lafleur, a member of the 1979 World Championships team, was a member of the Milwaukee Swiss Turners. Sandy Sobotka, a member of the USA National Team for three years, received her early training from the Turners in Chicago. These groups are very entrenched in their traditions and have not always kept pace with the mainstream of gymnastics at the highest levels, but they are still a viable and important force in gymnastics in America.

High schools have their own rules and regulations for competition in both men's and women's gymnastics. Often these rules vary from state to state. High school gymnastics training in recent years has been directed at the male athlete. Bart Conner is a former Illinois high school system all-around champion and many other male gymnasts were champions at various events in their high school programs. The women's programs are not quite as strong in the high schools. Most young women receive their training in private clubs or gyms that require payment of a tuition.

High schools do provide a large number of children with the ability to train, compete, and realize success. Moreover, high school stars are recipients of scholarships to some of the most prestigious universities in the land based upon their performance.

Many high schools are in a bit of a bind in gymnastics programs due to the problems of our economy and the expense of running a really top-notch program. Unfortunately, high school gymnastics programs have sometimes been cut in general budget trims. Gymnastics is not a high revenue-producing sport like football and basketball. The sport caters to a small number of people and the equipment is expensive. Therefore, when cuts have to be made, gymnastics may top the list.

A problem with some catastrophic, highly publicized injuries has also soured the high school community on gymnastics. In some cases, trampolines have been removed from schools. It has become difficult to locate qualified people to teach and coach gymnastics at the high school level.

The NCAA, or college, levels of gymnastics have been in existence for many years. It would be very difficult to find a male gymnast on an international team who has not been an NCAA athlete. There have been a few exceptions, however, and even now there is at least one male gymnast on the national team who competes with and for his club because his university does not have a gymnastics program.

The men's program at the college level is in jeopardy because the NCAA Division II program is to be eliminated after one more year due to an insufficient number of schools participating. The NCAA Division I already has less than the 7 percent of school participation that is required by NCAA rules.

The women's program is alive and well at the collegiate level and is, in fact, growing compared to the men's program. This is partly a result of the Title IX statutes (requiring public schools to guarantee equal opportunities in sports for both sexes) and partly because of increased interest.

The NCAA women's programs are becoming more and more competitive all the time. The last NCAA championships for women held at the University of Utah attracted over 17,000 spectators for a two-day tournament, which the University of Utah won for the second straight year. The scholarships available for young gymnasts entering collegiate competition are a tremendous boon to the growth of gymnastics.

Another member of the USGF is the USAIGC, the United States Association of Independent Gymnastics Clubs. The USAIGC was formed to meet the demands of the independent gymnastics school owner for an organization that saw to the needs and problems of this special combination of business and hobby. The independent club is a small business that offers gymnastics training and classes. Monthly tuitions vary from tens to hundreds of dollars. Clubs offer instruction to men and women of all ages. These clubs provide competition among themselves locally and through the USGF and USAIGC for state, regional, and national competitions. The USAIGC offers regional and national team championships and many special programs for the club owner to enhance his or her business and the ability to train the athletes to higher levels.

The USAIGC has also done a great deal to bring an added measure of professionalism to the full-time gymnastics coach by establishing standards for certification of coaches at all levels and outlets of participation. However, because the independent club is also a private business, some for profit and some not-for-profit, the moods and idiosyncracies of the business world have an effect on it and its ability to remain a viable institution.

The trend in athletics is to take high-level sport out of the public institutions and place it in the hands of the private sector. This is partly due to the inability of the public schools to do a better job, mostly because public schools cannot afford these programs and those likely to be attracted to high-level coaching are not always interested in being school teachers. These independent clubs are the result of this movement. There are close to 5,000 independent gymnastics clubs in the United States. While not all are affiliated with the USAIGC, they are similarly organized.

The various organizations offering gymnastics are important and viable institutions that continue to perform tremendous services for the sport, its participants and its spectators.

3

EVENTS FOR MEN
AND WOMEN

The actual competitive events for men and women have evolved through several stages.

Women currently compete in four events—vault, uneven parallel bars, balance beam, and floor exercise (Fig. 6). Generally, the events are scheduled in that order during a meet. Men compete in floor exercise, pommel horse, still rings, vault, parallel bars, and horizontal bar (Fig. 7) in that order. The designated order of events for both men and women is called the Olympic order. It was designed to maintain spectator interest, keep the gymnast safe, and ensure high-quality performances.

The women originally competed in the men's style of parallel bars before the development of "uneven" parallel bars, and on the flying rings, predecessor of our modern "still" rings.

The flying rings were two metal rings that were suspended from ropes. The gymnast performed on them as on the trapeze. As the gymnast hung onto the rings, a "thrower" would run holding the gymnast's feet, and propel him or her into a swing. Now, of course, only the male gymnast competes on the rings, and keeps them still during "hold" (stationary) parts of his routine.

Both men and women, from time to time, competed in "tumbling," the precursor to the fully developed floor exercise. It consisted of a series of passes or trips down a long strip of matting. There were requirements for tumbling forward, backward, and alternating tumbling of forward, backward, and sideward moves.

Another event was the rope climb. The gymnast would climb a specified length of rope without the use of his or her legs, racing against the clock.

The trampoline, at one time, was contested in the all-around. Although it remains one of America's first contributions to gymnastics apparatus, it has never been contested in the Olympic Games.

As the trampoline took hold in the United States, the National Collegiate Athletic Association offered competition in the event for some time. The trampoline was never widely accepted into the all-around program and, since the six events of men's gymnastics did not include trampoline in the Olympics, the push to develop the all-around gymnast and neglect the specialist caused the trampoline to slip a few notches in the list of priorities.

The trampoline eventually became considered a separate sport related to, but not contested, with gymnastics. The trampoline is still used today as a teaching tool for other phases of the sport. The trampoline offers several seconds of airborne freedom from gravity more difficult to obtain from other events. This helps gymnasts seeking to learn difficult aerial maneuvers.

A blow was handed to trampoline when the pediatric portion of the American Medical Association tried in September, 1977 to ban children's use of trampolines. This was the result of a high number of trampoline injuries involving permanent disability and paralysis. Although it was found that trampolining resulted in an inordinate amount of bad injuries, the trampoline was not taken out of use but went through a trial period to determine whether it could be made safer.

Unfortunately, trampolining has suffered severely. Schools have found it difficult to get insurance to defend themselves in the case of accidents involving the trampoline. Most schools have locked up or disposed of their trampolines.

The United States Gymnastics Safety Association in Washington, D.C. was founded to lobby for sound and ethical practices within the sport and support the gymnastics education profession. The association developed a safety manual and a regional and state testing program for instructors to add professionalism to teacher training in gymnastics, but it has been largely abandoned due to inertia and lack of funds.

The injury problem with the trampoline and the concern that gymnastics had been allowed to stray from providing healthy learning for children brought the inception of the National Gymnastics Catastrophic Injury Report at the University of Illinois. The third annual report of these investigations into case histories and patterns of gymnastics has shown a distinct drop in the number of serious injuries since 1978. Although limits to this report are freely acknowledged by the researchers, their work has been highly regarded.

The modern events for men and women came from a long period of evolution due to increased technology and the advent of some spectacular and difficult skills. Let's take a quick look at the various events to get an idea of what the gymnast must do and how equipment may have assisted the sport in its evolution.

U.S. national star Amy Koopman in a floor exercise routine.

Former U.S. national champion Kathy Johnson midway through a vault.

Fig. 6 **WOMEN'S EVENTS**

A competitor in the uneven bars.

Yumi Mordre on the balance beam in the Championships for the U.S.A.

Collegiate star Phil Cahoy on the pommel
horse.

Fig. 7　**MEN'S EVENTS.** *The men also perform the
floor exercise and vault.*

A Penn State athlete competing on the still rings.

Charles Lakes on the horizontal bar.

U.S. star Jim Hartung on the parallel bars.

WOMEN'S EVENTS

The Vault

The vaulting event is contested by both men and women. Women vault over a horse placed perpendicular to the run; men over a horse placed parallel to the run. The horse used in vaulting has the same configuration as the pommel horse for men except that it is higher for both men and women and the pommels are removed. The women's horse is about 4-and-a-half feet high. Since men vault lengthwise, over a horse that is 5-and-a-half feet high, the men's event is often called long-horse vaulting. The women vault with the horse sideward and therefore it is often called side-horse vaulting. Men are allowed about 20 meters, or 65 feet, for their run, wihich is limited by a toe board that does not allow the men to run further. Women are allowed approximately 78 feet for an approach.

The horse has been continually raised as the springiness of the vault boards, or takeoff boards, has increased and the higher level of difficulty has demanded more descent time (to accommodate more maneuvers) during the airborne portion of the vault from the horse to the landing. The vault board is the takeoff surface that the gymnast must hit with both feet to become airborne and reach the horse with his or her hands. The vaulting board itself has long been the source of controversy among coaches and athletes. Europeans have been slow to adopt the springier types of boards used in the United States. Since the FIG specification for the vaulting board requires that it be made out of wood, there were no metal spring boards in world competition until 1979, when the competition was held in the United States. Since then, European companies have been adopting the springier boards. The principal problem with wood, and the reason United States companies sought an alternative, is that the wood fibers fatigue rather quickly and the boards are expensive. The newer metal spring boards are less expensive and more durable.

The men's horse was originally divided into zones. Originally, the male gymnast often had to tell the judges which zones of the horse he was going to use. These zones have largely been eliminated and the gymnast simply needs to designate whether he is going to use the near end or the far end or both, as in the case of the Tsukahara vaults.

Women's horses do not have zones. However, the new vaults, in which the gymnast actually performs a skill on the takeoff board and then dives backward with or without twist to the horse, may result in some safety modifications of equipment. For example, the top surface may be widened so that the gymnast is less likely to miss it in between flights to and from the horse.

The vault is contested somewhat like track and field events. The gymnast's attempts are scored based on a 10.0 maximum total. Each vault is given a difficulty rating as in diving. Therefore, if the gymnast elects to do a very simple vault and performs it perfectly, he or she still may not win because another athlete performing a more difficult vault with some flaws might have the potential for reaching a higher score.

In women's gymnastics, the competitor is usually given two chances at the vault, with the better score counting. In the final rounds, however, the gymnast must do two different vaults and the scores are averaged.

In men's gymnastics, the athlete is given one attempt. It must count for the score. In finals, the men do two vaults and the scores are averaged. The scores are based on the difficulty of the vault as determined by the FIG or the governing body, the execution of the vault or those identifiable faults in performance, and the dynamics of the vault (how high and far the gymnast flew during the performance). There are even some set distances that the gymnast must travel to avoid being penalized.

The Uneven Parallel Bars

The uneven parallel bars were the outgrowth of the men's parallel bars that women originally used. The women were significantly limited in their ability to swing on parallel bars by relative upper body weakness. Their broader hips also made it harder to swing between the narrow rails. The uneven bars allow the female gymnast to perform on a hanging event without maintaining support for as long as the men, who tend to be stronger in the shoulders.

The uneven bars consist of two wood, or fiberglass, rails held high from the floor by metal uprights. The rails were not adjustable vertically in international competition until recently. The high bar may now be raised for exceptionally tall women. The horizontal distance between the bars may be changed to permit the gymnast to place the rails at the distance best suited to her performance. In some cases, the gymnast may wish to have the rails as far apart as possible to ease the mechanics of execution of a particular skill.

Small girls just learning gymnastics often use the uneven bars with adjustments for the width of the rails and height as well. Although this is discouraged in international competition, local and domestic competitions with very young gymnasts can usually accommodate many bar adjustments to facilitate the size of the young participant and the needs of the exercise.

The rails once looked like the men's parallel-bar rails (which are nearly rectangular with rounded edges), but have since become more and more rounded. They are quite flexible, permitting a wide variety of skills and methods for using them. The gymnast may use the low bar as a catapult by striking it on the front of her hips while grasping the high bar, which may be used in typical support fashion as in the men's high bar. The low bar is about 5 feet and the high bar about 7 and ½ feet from the floor.

The rail length is approximately 7 feet 9 inches. The bars are usually attached to the floor with an elaborate system of cables, pulleys, floor anchors, and tightening mechanisms. These contribute to high-level performances by providing the gymnast with a "spring" rail to work with. The old wooden rails have been largely abandoned as the level of difficulty on the bars has increased; the wood tended to dry out, resulting in cracked and damaged rails. At times, the gymnast actually smashed right through them during the execution of some large swings. With the increased use of the fiberglass rail, this danger has become virtually non-existent.

The uneven parallel bars are usually considered the most daring of the women's events. This is especially true with the advent of large swinging skills and the releases and regrasps that have been the trademark of good uneven-bar work. A gymnast's seemingly reckless swings and releases followed by some somersault or twist in the air to arrive back on the bars again and move freely into another skill typify the elegance and the daring of the uneven bars. The routine should consist of ten or eleven skills as defined by the Federation of International Gymnastics (FIG). During the routine, the competitor should use both bars, change directions, perform swinging skills without stopping, and release and regrasp the bars. The routine must have a mount, or a special skill designed to get on the apparatus, and a dismount, which is an equally special skill. In between, the gymnast must fly with the daring of a wombat and the skill of a monkey.

The Balance Beam

The balance beam has changed little in the evolution of gymnastics—at least in general concept. The beam was still made of wood with no covering as late as 1972. Olga Korbut has received most of the credit for causing the beam to be padded and covered when she did the back somersault on it in the Olympic Games in Munich.

The beam is 10 centimeters wide, which is slightly less than four inches. The length of the beam is approximately 16½ feet; the top is roughly four feet from the floor. The beam usually consists of a hardwood top surface with a rubberized absorptive material only a few millimeters thick underneath. The remaining beam structure is composed of wood. Aluminum beams with padding are a recent development. The advantages of aluminum are that it doesn't warp and can be manufactured with more consistency and less expense.

Again, in the various age group programs the beam may be set at a variety of heights to accommodate the skills and safety needs of the gymnast. The beam exercise has a time limit: the same as for the women's floor exercise (from 1 minute 10 seconds to 1 minute and 30 seconds). A gymnast who falls off the beam must remount in five seconds or the routine is terminated at that point. There is also a warning tone, or buzzer, to tell the gymnast she has only five seconds in which to dismount without deduction and another tone to announce the end of time.

The balance beam exercise is basically floor exercise on a high and narrow plank without music. The routine usually has handstands and the more noteworthy tricks of gymnastics, such as somersaults and flips. It also must have various skills from the dance areas like turns, leaps, jumps, and body waves. The combination of these skills is what makes balance beam and gymnastics so unusual in its character. The dance offers elegance and rhythm, and is a medium for mood and characterization. Gymnastics adds to this the element of risk, danger, athleticism, and competition.

The balance beam is the great equalizer in women's gymnastics. The skills on the beam are not necessarily very difficult from a learning and performance standpoint. The same skills done on the floor are quite simple. However, performing these skills on the beam, with the small margin for error with such a narrow surface, is what makes the beam a high-pressure event. Many an all-around has been lost due to one tiny miscalculation on the balance beam.

The narrow beam provides great potential for elegance and beauty and, with that, a commensurate amount of risk and anxiety. Unfortunately, for artistry the balance beam has also gone the route of floor exercise as winning has become so paramount that simply avoiding errors is the name of the game. Few risks are taken on skills other than those necessary to accomplish the combination requirements. Each event must contain a certain number of difficult skills, a number of intermediate difficult skills, and some connecting moves. In attempting to gain the most difficulty points with the least amount of risk, most of the beam routines are now relegated to acrobatics punctuated only with the most simple and unadorned dance simply to prepare for the next acrobatic series. We hope this trend will change, but the event will probably become more acrobatic before it becomes more artistic.

Floor Exercise

Men and women both compete in floor exercise. This event is contested first in the men's order and last in the women's. Women perform to music. Men must perform their routine or exercise in 50 to 70 seconds and the women from one minute, ten seconds to one minute, 30 seconds. A tone signals the gymnast when he has five seconds left in international men's competition.

Both the men's and women's events use a tone to tell gymnasts when they are over their limits.

The floor exercise area is currently a large, square, matted area that measures 10 meters square or roughly 40 feet by 40 feet. The area is now padded but, in the recent past, the gymnasts competed on the hard gymnasium floor with no matting at all. The area of the floor exercise is bounded by a white line. It must not be overstepped by the gymnast or he or she will receive a deduction from the final score.

The modern floor exercise area is really a masterpiece of modern technology. The floor areas now are usually "spring floors." These spring floors are made through a variety of techniques. Some use actual metal springs—about 50 for each 4 × 8 sheet of plywood. The springs rest on the floor and support the plywood so that the gymnast gets the added impulse of the spring on take-offs for tumbling skills. The gymnast also receives cushioning during landings. There are other varieties of spring floors that use special kinds of foam under the wood sections.

Above the wood is a mat surface, usually an inch or so thick, to provide a softer and more comfortable surface upon which to tumble, roll, and dance. The final and most visible layer of the spring floor is usually carpet or vinyl. This is the actual surface on which the gymnast tumbles. These new spring floors have brought a significant increase in difficulty to gymnastics for men and women and a much-needed addition of safety to tumbling. The increased comfort of tumbling, the extra spring of takeoffs, and the added "forgiveness" of the surface on landings makes the modern spring floor one of the greatest additions to gymnastics since chalk, which helps gymnasts maintain their grip on bar events. One coach remarked that his gymnasts' careers will last five more years as a result of spring floors.

The floor exercise event must consist of tumbling and other gymnastics skills. In men's floor exercise, these are sometimes called corner moves. In women's gymnastics these other skills include the dance portions and the other slower-moving or stationary tumbling skills, such as handstands.

The routine should consist of several tumbling passes punctuated with exciting and dramatic dance and/or stationary skills that demonstrate strength, balance, flexibility, acrobatics, etc. The routine should carry its difficulty level throughout the exercise. In other words, the gymnast should not start out with all his or her hard skills and then do little of difficulty at the end. The difficulty should be balanced throughout the routine. The gymnast must also perform the routine using all of the exercise area, including corners, side, and middle.

In the case of the music for women, there has been a radical change since 1979 when orchestrated music was allowed as opposed to the single instrument, almost always piano, that had been used in the past. The addition of orchestrated music had a much more profound influence by sheer volume, if nothing else, on the character of floor exercise as well as the fun of performing it.

Finally, the routine should form a single entity. The rules often use words such as "harmonious," "rhythmic," and "whole," to describe floor exercise. The routine should not only consist of several skills executed in succession but it should also be able to be viewed in its entirety like a well-choreographed dance or short story.

The escalation of difficulty to such high levels and the need for safety, plus the inherent desires of most athletes and coaches to win at all costs, has de-emphasized much of this artistry in recent years. The coaches and athletes know that to win they usually must simply avoid mistakes or deductions. Unfortunately, this has brought a kind of sterility to floor exercise that is usually only avoided by the most bold and gifted of athletes. The goal of winning above artistry has brought us greater levels of difficulty, but as the gymnasts try and outdo each other in the beauty of the engineering of the skills, they have lost much of the insight needed to make a truly artistic performance.

MEN'S EVENTS

We have already discussed the men's vault and floor exercise. The remaining events are the pommel horse, still rings, parallel bars, and horizontal bar.

The Pommel Horse

The pommel horse has two wooden pommels, or handles, on the top. The pommel horse is about three feet and eight inches to the top of the vinyl surface and the pommels are about five inches tall. They have recently been made flat on the top; earlier pommels were rounded or crowned. The pommel horse is a little over five feet long. The top surface is usually treated or covered differently from the sides so that the gymnast has a good grip and feel for the top vinyl areas. The sides are usually kept smooth to promote easy sliding of the legs during the exercise. The pommel horse may be clamped to the floor to prevent movement and shaking, but in the United States, we usually simply make the base very heavy so that the horse does not move during the routine.

The pommel horse exercise consists primarily of two types of swing. The type that forms the bulk of the routine is the circular swing in which the gymnast has both legs together and swings his feet in a wide, flat, horizontal circle around his hands and support. The second type of swing is the pendular or scissor swing in which the gymnast swings from side to side, usually with one leg on the forward side of the horse and one leg on the backward side.

The intricacies of the pommel horse exercises are considerable. Even judges have trouble recognizing them because of the quick execution and incredibly tough combinations of consecutive difficult skills.

The pommel horse is the great equalizer for men. It is usually recognized as being the most difficult apparatus since the ever-changing support of the hands makes accuracy crucial and difficult. The slightest miscalculation of swing usually produces a fall and loss of contention.

Pommel horse also provides one of the most dramatic events in all of the sport. The pressure is usually tremendous. The worker glides through a routine in near silence with such intricate maneuvers that most cannot even follow the sequence. Dismounting and standing perfectly still highlight the special drama that belongs to few sports.

The Still Rings

The still rings represent one of the two "hanging" events for men. (The pommel horse is a support event since the gymnast must constantly maintain his body above his hands.) In fact, the gymnast using still rings is in support during a part of the routine, but since the swing portions of the exercise usually predominate, the rings are considered a hanging event.

The rings are made of laminated wood or fiberglass and suspended from straps of leather or nylon webbing. The strap is, in turn, suspended from a cable connected to swivel bearings on either a ring suspension frame or the ceiling. In most big meets, the rings are suspended from this ring frame. The actual height of the ends of the cables must be consistent due to the physical laws of the pendulums that the rings and the gymnast must obey during a performance. The bottoms of the rings are about 8½ feet from the floor and the cables are suspended from the ring frame at about 18 feet from the floor. The height of the rings is important because the athlete must always count on the same amount of airborne time during dismounts and to avoid hitting the floor with his feet as he swings fully extended. The length of the cable is also important because the period of the pendular swing of the ring cables and the rings themselves can have a profound effect on the ability of the gymnast to perform his large swinging skills consistently and accurately. Interestingly, the exercise known as the "iron cross" that the typical lay person regards as the trademark of the male ring gymnast is much easier if the cables are significantly shorter.

The ring tower or frame itself is usually guyed by cables and sometimes tubing to make the frame very steady. The ring frame is usually preferable to suspending the rings from a rafter in the ceiling since the ring frame has a natural "give" to it during swing and rafters don't. This give, or bend, makes the swinging forces much easier on the gymnast's shoulders and joints than the rings suspended from an absolutely solid object.

Performance consists of skills that have the gymnast swing during support (i.e., when the gymnast's body is above his hands) and during a hang. The gymnast should arrive at a handstand on the rings by both swing and strength. But strength is the major contributor to success in the still rings and is most appreciated by the lay person.

Positions that show the remarkable strength and precision of the gymnast are most clearly seen on the still rings. The simple strength that is needed to support yourself on the rings can, at first, be a tremendous accomplishment. The rare combination of strength and skill through swing is the most beautiful concept of the event. To swing with apparent abandon only to arrive in a perfectly still handstand or cross position is one of the really eye-pleasing moments in gymnastics. The rings are unusual in that the gymnast does not let go of the apparatus until the dismount.

Dismounts provide the gymnast that short-lived opportunity to cut the bonds of gravity and perform some highly intricate or graceful maneuver before gravity takes over again and brings him to a perfectly still and controlled landing on the floor.

The Parallel Bars

The parallel bars are one of the oldest pieces of apparatus and one of the most underrated. The parallel bars are two wooden or fiberglass rails set parallel to each other and about 5 feet, 9 inches from the floor. The bars are about 11 feet long and are adjustable both vertically and horizontally. The gymnast works the bars usually parallel to their length but can also work the bars like men's horizontal bar or women's uneven bars.

The routine must consist of swinging movements that work above and below the bar; therefore it is both a support and hanging event. The gymnast usually performs somersaults, leg swings, handstands, and, of course, the mount and dismount. The routine consists of about eleven skills and the gymnast should show flights, swings, and releases. The routine can include skills entirely from the strength category such as presses to handstands and planches (in which the gymnast, using only his hands, raises or lowers his body to the horizontal). The gymnast might also elect to show ability in balance by balancing on one rail or one hand. The parallel bars are also usually one of the first events for the young male gymnast to enjoy and master.

The Horizontal Bar

The horizontal bar is perhaps the most spectacular and awe-inspiring event in the sport.

The horizontal bar is made of specially tempered steel and sits about 8½ feet off the floor. The bar is held up with vertical uprights that are cabled into the floor for stability. The bar is about 8 feet long. The gymnast swings around the bar with large, fully stretched body positions called, aptly enough, "giant swings" and close to the bar with smaller swinging movements.

The horizontal bar is last in the men's order of Olympic events and rightly so since it forms a really grand finale to any competition. The gymnast must swing about the bar in both directions with changes of grip and with large and small swings. He must release the bar and regrasp it again and his dismount must be at least as difficult as the rest of the skills in the routine. The horizontal bar requires the gymnast to swing around the bar in an "elgrip," "dorsal," or "cubital" grip. These swings are vitally important to the gymnast, but somewhat difficult for the lay person to understand.

The elgrip, similar to the "Eagle grip" used by women on the uneven bars, is performed with the hands in reverse, or "chin-up" grip on the bar. As the gymnast swings forward, his arms, relative to his body, move back, upward, and overhead, and the shoulders go through gymnastic dislocation. Not only does the gymnast have to hang in this grip, but he must also support himself in the handstand in this grip. This is hard. The dorsal grip is similar to the way you might see young children hang in the "skin the cat" position from monkey bars in the playground. The child hangs from the bar using a regular "pull-up" grip and puts both legs between his or her hands in a tucked, hanging position. Then, the child keeps turning over backward without letting go until he or she is fully stretched, hanging onto the bar with the back facing the bar and feet near the ground. The cubital grip is performed in a swing known as a Czech giant. The gymnast places his hands in a regular "pull-up" position on the bar, and as he swings forward, his arms, relative to his body, move upward, forward, and then backward, to produce what is known as anatomic inlocation.

The recent addition of spectacular releases to the men's horizontal bar has made the event most exciting and risky. The gymnast not only swings around the bar, but now must let go of the bar, perform a somersault, or turn and return to the bar. The horizontal bar routine is always ended with a dismount. Dismounts are becoming more and more spectacular as the gymnasts perform not only double but triple somersaults. In fact, double somersaults with multiple twists are almost becoming commonplace.

Perhaps the most unusual twist to the horizontal bar is the "one-arm giant," where the participant swings around the bar using only one hand for gripping. This does not seem incredible until you consider that the gymnast will have forces on his hands to the measure of 5 to 7 times his body weight per square inch on the bottom of the swings. It's a wonder he can even hang on, much less perform skills! But perform them he does, as there are dismounts being done from one-arm giants and all matter of releases and regrasps, turns, and swings.

THE ALL-AROUND

The final event in modern artistic gymnastics is perhaps the most important. This is the all-around. In gymnastics, along with the team titles, the most coveted prize is the all-around championship. The all-around is decided much like the decathlon in track and field in that the athletes' total score from all the events is all that is necessary. However, unlike the decathlon, there is a lot of importance also placed on the individual event champions, since the gymnast could win a single event or several events but may not win the all-around.

The all-around is a measure of general competence as shown on all the events. It also means that the gymnast can excel without winning every single event.

NEW FOR '84 OLYMPICS:

RHYTHMIC GYMNASTICS

Modern rhythmic gymnastics, or as it is usually called, rhythmic gymnastics, is a new sport for the 1984 Olympics. It promises to add a very new and very different flavor to Olympic and related gymnastics competition (Fig. 8).

The rhythmic gymnast is a cross between a ballerina, acrobat, contortionist, and juggler. Rhythmic gymnastics is at least as old as its counterpart, artistic gymnastics, but uses lighter hand implements instead of the heavy apparatus familiar to many of us from television coverage of previous games.

The rhythmic gymnast competes in an area, which is exactly the size of the floor exercise mat, but which doesn't need to be padded. The gymnast uses one of five hand apparatuses: balls, ropes, hoops, ribbons, or Indian clubs. The

Fig. 8 *Rhythmic Gymnastics: New for the '84 Olympics.*

balls are a little larger than a typical softball, the rope is the size of a typical jump rope, the hoops are similar to the old hula hoop, the ribbon consists of a small wooden stick to one end of which is attached a long and usually multi-colored ribbon that streams through the air, and, finally, the Indian clubs resemble skinny bowling pins.

The gymnast performs a dance and light acrobatic routine in the floor exercise area to music. At this point, only the piano is used. The gymnast should show dance skills, turns, jumps, leaps, hops, body waves, and arm movements—all in unison with the music and utilizing the hand apparatus much as a magician might use a silk handkerchief to show grace. The gymnasts both throw the implements in the air about their bodies and throw their bodies in the air about the implements.

Although rhythmic gymnastics has a more than 20-year history of competition in Europe, the event is still relatively new in the United States. Largely because the rhythmic gymnast must rely upon dance technique for competence, this event has had a relatively small following and even less understanding. World Championships have existed in rhythmic gymnastics since 1963 and the Eastern bloc countries have easily dominated.

The major differences between artistic and rhythmic gymnastics is that only women compete in the rhythmic event. There are also no flips, handstands, round-offs, or walkovers allowed in rhythmic gymnastics. The rhythmic gymnast may do rolls, splits, and other contortionistic poses on her seat, stomach, chest, or shoulders, and she may pass inverted as long as she does not pass through the vertical. In other words, she may not perform a skill in which she moves upside-down and completes a 180-degree turn, such as a cartwheel.

The skills in rhythmic gymnastics are rated in difficulty but are not very similar to those in standard gymnastics. Each routine must contain eight elements of difficulty, of which at least two must be of superior difficulty. At least three of the eight skills must be performed with the nondominant hand, or the gymnast receives a penalty. Examples of elements of difficulty include throwing clubs overhead, juggling them, passing them behind the back, and using one or two clubs at a time; tossing and spinning hoops, or juggling them, etc. Each implement gives rise to its own group of movements, and the gymnast should demonstrate a wide variety of them in her routine. Penalties are sustained if the gymnast drops her implement, fails to keep the implement in motion, moves out of time to the music, or demonstrates bad form in her dance elements.

Competition is done singly with one gymnast performing her routine to music and for specific time limits, or as a group exercise consisting of six gymnasts performing a choreographed routine in which all the participants throw and catch the implements, dance, jump, and leap—sometimes in unison, sometimes alone, and always with such elegance and beauty that modern rhythmic gymnastics is an impressive, beautiful addition to the Olympic events.

4

PERFORMANCE
AND JUDGING

WHAT MAKES A COMPETITIVE EXERCISE?

What is different about the gymnastics you might have done in physical education class or that young children practice in the yard? The circus often has acrobats doing skills that look a lot like the gymnastics you see on television or perhaps do yourself. What is different about what a Chinese acrobatic team does and what Kurt Thomas and Nadia Comaneche do? Let's begin with a look at the way a competitive exercise is developed and evaluated. The competitive exercise is, of course, different for each event. But there are certain elements that the exercises have in common.

The various levels of gymnastics and different governing bodies make understanding the competitive exercise a little more difficult. Participants may score better with the same exercise at one level than another, for reasons we'll soon see. This is because nearly all the different skills in gymnastics have been named and carry a point value that indicates their difficulty, and degree of originality or virtuosity.

The difficulty value of the skill is important to the competitive exercise, because the gymnast must have skills from certain difficulty levels in order to receive a representative score. Knowing the difficulty of all the skills is a lifelong occupation. Judges must study constantly simply to keep abreast. This is an especially tough job, of course, since the difficulty of the skills may be different from one region to another.

Originality, one of the most important parts of the competitive exercise, is difficult for the lay person to assess. A knowledge of what is usual is needed before one can tell what is rare or original. The gymnast seeks to include original skills for point increases and for pride of accomplishment. The virtuosity of the skill is something that the lay person can understand and appreciate, for instance, feats such as flying very high on a vault, landing in a handstand, or showing such ease and control that the audience truly gets the impression that the skill was performed with no effort.

Another important facet of the competitive exercise is the evaluation provided by the judging organizations. The gymnast must observe earlier competition to know what the judges are looking to reward with high scores. The coach and the athlete work toward the test and most training is directed specifically toward fulfilling the rules' requirements so that the competitive routine or exercise will receive higher scores.

The competitive exercise must then satisfy two requirements: the personal artistic requirements of the athlete and coach, and the compositional requirements defined by the governing body in charge of evaluation.

The individual routines are composed of skills that fit together with a beginning, middle, and end. The individual skills are all rated for difficulty with a triad scaling of A, B, and C. The A's are easier, lower level difficulty skills. The B's are medium difficulty skills. The C's are high level difficulty skills. Each skill has been rated by this ABC method. If the judge sees a new skill for the first time, he or she uses the three-level structure of evaluation to give the skill a difficulty evaluation.

A gymnast is assigned 10.00 points at the beginning of the routine, from which points are deducted for errors in execution and composition. A portion of the 10.00 points is devoted to the number and difficulty of skills being performed in the routine. Each routine must have a certain number of C's, B's, and A's, a proportion that changes depending on the competition. Individual event finals have more stringent requirements (i.e., they must contain more high-difficulty skills) than all-around or preliminary competitions.

Vaulting is scored differently from the other exercises, as we have explained earlier. Each vault is rated on a 0 to 10 scale, with more difficult vaults given higher values. The gymnast performs different or higher level vaults as the competition increases in prestige and difficulty.

Women's Events

Here are a few simple ideas for evaluating gymnastics exercises. Complete understanding of the event requires a knowledge of the material surrounding the routines. The idiosyncracies of judging will be left for another section.

Vaults are categorized into families and given a point value. There are three principal families of vaults designated by score, those with a maximum value up to 9.0, those valued 9.0–9.5, and those valued from 9.5 to 10.0.

The families are distinguished by the number of twists, number of somersaults, degree of stretch of the body in the flight from the horse to the landing, or a combination of all of these elements. For example, a simple handspring vault is valued at 8.8 points; a handspring with a full twist is valued at 9.4; a handspring with a double twist is valued at 10.0 points.

All vaults that contain both a somersault and a twist are in the 9.5 to 10.0 score range but differ in score value. A handspring followed by a 1 and ½ front somersault in a tuck position (in which the knees are brought up to the chest during flight) is worth a maximum of 9.7. If the gymnast adds a half twist to the above vault, the score then is worth a maximum of 9.8. If she does the vault with a half twist and in the pike (in which the body is bent at the waist and the legs are straight), rather than the tuck position, the vault is worth a maximum of 9.9.

Scoring based on the number of twists and somersaults is relatively self-explanatory. The more skilled gymnast can get more somersaulting or twisting done in the short airborne period. The more skill it takes to perform the vault, the more difficult it is and therefore the higher score it should earn.

There are three different body positions in the vault: tuck, pike, and layout. The more stretched the body is the more force, therefore skill, it takes to complete the turns or somersault. This need for extra force diminishes the margin for error, makes the vault more difficult, and therefore merits a higher point value. The layout position, in which the body is completely straight, is the most difficult body position in the vaults; the tuck position is the easiest.

After the gymnast has elected to perform a vault with a specific value, there are other criteria that contribute to his or her score. The gymnast who flies higher and farther from the horse should receive the better score. The gymnast who lands solidly should score higher than one with a wobbly landing. The gymnast who keeps her knees straight or legs together (unless these positions are required by the vault itself) should receive a higher score. The vault should be straight, with the gymnast landing directly in front of the horse, not off to the sides. The run is not supposed to be judged at all, but it is evaluated indirectly since a faster and more efficient run generally produces a better vault. The hands should be placed on the horse accurately. Any cheating (deliberately placing the hands in the wrong place) or misalignment of hands receives a deduction.

The uneven bars are very difficult for judges to evaluate because of the routine's speed and the variety of combinations that can be performed. Although there are some significant exceptions, movements about the thighs and hands (such as a cast) are usually easier unless there are high flights or releases and somersaulting. Movements circling the bar from the hands only (such as a free hip circle) are generally one step up in difficulty, especially those swings that depart from, or arrive in, handstands.

Movements from bar to bar that do not involve somersaulting are a much broader category of skills, and may involve some very difficult moves (as when the gymnast moves from one bar to another to land in a handstand or hang).

Somersaulting skills from bar to bar are easier to evaluate. Skills involving twists look deceptively easy, but are in fact quite difficult. Those skills in which the gymnast somersaults and catches the same bar represent a newer and more sophisticated degree of bar work and a very high degree of difficulty.

A routine should contain about ten or eleven skills. The gymnast must work both bars and change directions. Deductions occur when the gymnast brushes the ground during the routine, or falls to the floor or onto the bars themselves. Deductions also result when the gymnast touches the bars with part of her body not supposed to be used for a particular skill, or when she does not swing to a full handstand. The gymnast should work quickly. No stops are allowed and she should dismount solidly. There is no time limit for the uneven bars, but a gymnast who falls from the apparatus has only thirty seconds in which to continue or the routine is considered terminated. The gymnast who falls can return to where she broke the routine in any fashion without getting additional deductions. She cannot begin her run more than eighteen feet from the bars. The coach is not allowed to stand between the bars, touch, make signals, or talk to the gymnast.

The bars can sometimes be adjusted vertically to suit the competitor's size. In the United States, that means different things at different levels of competitions. At some levels, the gymnast can adjust the high and low bars vertically and horizontally. In international competition, however, the gymnast must be over 5 feet, 5 inches in order to change the bars up and down.

If the gymnast sets the bars in the wrong place before mounting, she may not repeat the routine. If, however, the gymnast is distracted by something beyond her control, she then can usually repeat the exercise if she wants to after asking the superior judge. Such a distraction might be a failure of the equipment or a flashbulb from the spectators.

The balance beam must be contested during a time period of one minute, ten seconds to one minute, thirty seconds. There are supposed to be ten or eleven elements of difficulty, but the spectator may be befuddled by all the "extra dance" movements (Fig. 9).

The balance beam is composed of dance, balance, and tumbling skills. The tumbling skills are easily recognizable—handsprings, walkovers, somersaults, flips, etc. The more skills shown without stopping, the more difficult the routine is considered. The balance skills include handstands, handstands with turns, stands on one foot in a variety of positions, and sitting, standing, and lying positions.

The dance skills consist of leaps, jumps, hops, turns, and various combinations of these with rhythm and elegance. The typical American spectator may not understand the difficulty of the dance skills, which are often more difficult than the easily recognizable tumbling skills. Dancing can usually be under-

Fig. 9 *Mary Lou Retton on the beam—performing a skill in practice and in public are two different things.*

stood generally by looking at a few factors. The more turns, the more difficult the routine. The more that eye focus must be taken away from the beam, the more difficult. And, the more rapid the movements, the more difficult.

The gymnast who falls off the beam suffers a .5 deduction, and that's pretty expensive. The gymnast has five seconds in which to remount the beam after falling.

The gymnast receives most of her deductions from balance errors, which include body movements to regain balance, stopping the routine to regain balance, and grasping the beam to stay on. The mount onto the balance beam is usually some variation of a handstand and the dismount is generally a somersault. The more skills that the gymnast chains together quickly, and without stopping, and the more twists and somersaults in the dismount, the more difficult the routine.

The floor exercise event is composed of dance and tumbling. Although most of the actual time is spent dancing, tumbling skills are the most recognizable.

The more height and sureness, the better the score should be. These skills are not as easily recognizable for difficulty, but the more turns, altitude, and changes of body positions, the more difficult the routine.

The gymnast must perform with perfect synchronization to the music or face deductions. The music is an important facet of women's floor exercise. It should help her express an idea, an image, and her personality.

The floor exercise must last from 1 minute, 10 seconds to 1 minute, 30 seconds. The gymnast usually uses three tumbling passes. She generally takes a short dance sequence before her first tumbling pass to avoid fatigue. She again dances shortly before the second tumbling pass, also to avoid fatigue. This is followed by the longest dance sequence and generally a large change of rhythm allowing her to slow down and rest before the last tumbling pass. The last pass usually runs very close to the end of the music, when the gymnast again dances for a short sequence to end the routine with the end of the music.

Men's Events

The men begin on floor exercise for a routine of 50 to 70 seconds. The gymnast generally begins with a series of tumbling skills that move across a diagonal route from one corner of the exercise arena to the opposite corner. Then, the gymnast might return along the same diagonal for his second pass or he might do his required "side" pass by moving along the side edge of the mat to a different corner. There are usually three or four tumbling passes.

The gymnast follows with strength and balance skills. He usually satisfies both requirements by doing a press or slow moving skill that begins close to the mat and ends in the handstand position. The press should be done with an even rhythm since any jerkiness or unnecessary hand movements receive deductions. Then, the competitor usually uses the handstand and subsequent movements to turn around, followed by more tumbling or perhaps a balance on one foot before the tumbling. The gymnast must then perform the last tumbling pass to end in a "stuck," or solid landing.

Tumbling should include skills that flip and twist, or both at the same time. The gymnast who successfully performs somersaulting skills that have more twists per flip is more likely to receive a higher score. The gymnast who performs a larger number of flips or does them with a more stretched body position is generally performing a more difficult skill and receives more credit. Unlike women's gymnastics, where the landing during the exercise can be danced, the male gymnast usually must land motionless after his aerial somersaulting.

The male gymnast does not perform to music, although he should show a rhythmic quality to his work. Elegance generally gives way to raw power in the men's floor exercise, but of course the more elegant gymnast who is also performing high-level tumbling will generally win.

The pommel horse is competed next in the Olympic order. It consists of "circular" swings and swings that move one leg on alternating sides of the horse in "scissors." The routine must consist of swings of one and both legs that cover all parts of the horse. As you face the horse from the side, the end to the left is called the croupe or rear of the horse. The middle (between the pommels) is called the saddle. The right end is the neck. The gymnast must touch, or work, all three parts of the horse during his routine. He should alternately face both directions and should do some of the swings with his hands behind his back. He must never stop during the exercise and he may only touch the horse and pommels with his hands.

The better exercises show the gymnast swinging in more extended positions. The higher the legs swing in the circular and scissor swings, the higher the score.

The height of the swings, avoiding of touching the horse with the legs, working with the hands behind the back, and combining the skills in the most difficult manner mark the accomplished gymnast. The gymnast who can turn his torso in the opposite direction or form a clearly-outlined circle with his legs is generally more skilled and the smoother the swings are, the more accomplished the athlete is.

The still rings are the next event for men. The gymnast begins with a perfectly still hang and ends with a dismount that brings him to a perfectly still stand.

The gymnast must swing and move to a handstand and show strength skills like the "cross." There are many other skills that demonstrate strength on the rings; some appear deceptively easy. In general, the farther the rings are from his body, the more difficult the position. The longer the gymnast stays in position, the stronger he is.

The gymnast will move the position of the rings during his swinging movements, but must have them absolutely still when he stops swinging and attempts hold or press movements. Any movement of the rings during a hold position causes deductions. If the gymnast does not hold a position long enough or bends his arms or legs, this also results in deductions.

The gymnast who swings with the straightest arms, through the most extended positions, and shows the most still and strong hold positions is usually the winner. The dismount should always end in an upright and still landing.

The vault is the next event for men. The men compete on the long-horse vault, in which they jump over the horse body lengthwise. The pommels on the pommel horse are never used in vaulting. The men take a fast run on approach to the board and take off from both feet to land on the horse with one or both hands. The gymnast uses his hands to push the horse forcefully and create a high afterflight, during which he performs a twisting or somer-saulting skill—or both.

The higher and farther the gymnast flies before landing, the better. The more solidly the gymnast can land in the center of the mat, the better. The more twisting and somersaulting, the better. And, the more extended the gymnast is, the better.

The next event for men is the parallel bars. They can be performed with only swinging skills if the gymnast desires, but he must show some handstand positions and some releases. He may also elect to show some hold parts and strength movements. The gymnast whose parallel bar routine contains swings and releases that land surely and exactly in the handstand usually shows better skill. The gymnast who can perform a variety of swings above and below the bars can also receive higher scores. Finally, the gymnast should perform a dismount that involves twisting, somersaulting, or both.

The last event for men is the horizontal bar. The gymnast, with extended body positions, must swing with large movements that are close to the bar. He should change directions and use a variety of grips and releases. The better high bar workers swing extended, change directions many times, swing with one hand on the bar, and perform releases in which they fly high above the bar to turn and somersault before regrasping the bar again (Fig. 10).

The gymnast who swings with the most daring skills, does the highest dismount, and shows the most precision generally wins.

The most common deductions in the events result if the gymnast: fails to show enough skills, loses the grip and subsequent fluidity of movement, or falls.

Fig. 10 *A gymnast chalks up to ensure a proper grip.*

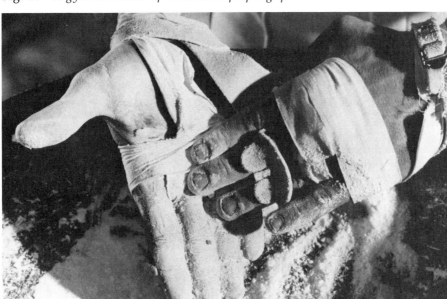

WHAT ARE COMPULSORY EXERCISES?

Compulsory exercises are routines required by one or more of the governing bodies of a particular gymnastics event. In most cases, each athlete must do them.

The compulsories for international competition, as we discussed earlier, are designed to be used over a four-year span each Olympiad. At the end of the Olympiad, they are discarded and new ones are designed and implemented for the next four-year period. Every four years, different countries are given the responsibility of coming up with the new compulsory exercise for a given event.

Being selected as the country with the responsibility of designing compulsories may be politically advantageous, since that country's individual athletes will know early what the exercises will be and thus can gain extra training time. The country may also be able to design a compulsory that hides its athletes' weaknesses.

The compulsory exercises are designed by the better minds in gymnastics from each selected country and then submitted to the technical committees of the FIG (Federation of International Gymnastics) for approval. The implementation of the compulsories is a big job. The text must be written in several languages. The actual wording can be very difficult since each subtle movement of the gymnast must be described in detail so there is no confusion. There are also revisions and interpretations. The routines are sent in written form, an artist draws a cartoon of each position, and films are made to show the intent of the compulsory.

The age-group compulsories in the United States are applied to all four levels of competition in the USGF (U.S. Gymnastics Federation) age-group program: class IV, class III, class II, and class I. The Elite compulsories are always the current Olympic compulsories as designated by the FIG.

The age-group compulsories in the United States are done as in the FIG format. The compulsories are usually given out through a special committee to certain people to design them. Usually they are given skills that the committee would like to see in the compulsories. However, the actual composition is left to the authors of the routines.

Age-group compulsories are usually developmental. As the gymnast progresses, he or she will be able to move from the previous to a higher level compulsory with relative ease. In other words, each age-level compulsory should build upon the previous age or ability level. Designing routines to fit the special needs of each level and performer is a thankless and nearly impossible job.

The compulsory routines are also often a source of frustration for athlete and spectator. They seldom get much press coverage, since they are usually not considered as appealing to the spectators as the optional exercises. Therefore, it may be difficult for the spectator to keep track of the scores, even up to the finals. However, compulsories usually account for 50% of the gymnast's score.

Not all members of the gymnastics world do compulsories, but all high-level international competitions, including the Olympic Games, World Championships, and Pan-American Games, do. There are relatively few international invitationals that use them, however, and movements have been afoot lately to remove compulsories from the international program.

The limited use of compulsories is largely due to expense. The competition hall must be procured for one or two more days, and judges must be housed and paid for these extra days. The gymnasts must also be housed and fed for a longer period.

Compulsory exercises in the United States age-group program are firmly entrenched, but the NCAA only requires the male all-around performers to do compulsories. The NCAA women's competition doesn't use them at all.

Let's look at the reasons for using compulsories so we may better appreciate what they are and what they do.

Compulsory routines have counterparts in other sports. The figure skater does school figures or patch, and the diver has required dives. The "performance" types of sports are the ones most likely to use "compulsory" types of skills to evaluate the athlete. The compulsory forces evaluation on criteria that apply to each athlete and provide an additional means of evaluation.

The compulsory also provides another set of scores to use in differentiating the ranks of competitors. This does not seem like much of a reason until you consider the really practical problems of having many athletes with rather similar abilities together. For example, in the 1981 World Championships on men's horizontal bar, there were four "tens" awarded. One of the gymnasts who received this perfect mark of ten in the finals did not receive even a bronze medal. How did this happen? His compulsory and preliminary scores were not as high as the others.

When gymnasts are very good, all of their scores will fall in the 9.4 to the 9.9 range. This does not leave much room to distinguish the best athlete. The judges need finer distinctions to put the gymnasts in rank order, but the rules only allow for differentiations of tenths of a point. For instance, the all-around may often be won by one-tenth of a point. This makes each tenth very valuable and makes the job of the judges particularly critical. Since the scores usually end up close at each ability level, compulsories provide more opportunity for the gymnasts to obtain more deductions from their total scores and spread out the scores.

If this did not happen, the number of ties that could occur in the women's all-around would be high since there are only four events in which to gain a lead and maintain it. The extra four or six routines that compulsories provide help differentiate the ranks of the gymnasts more clearly and sometimes represent the only differences.

The second use for compulsories is educational. The goals of the compulsory are to provide a "forced" training in certain basic skills that the governing body or other experts would like to see improved or to help manipulate the direction of gymnastics through the careful selection of skills. The concept of forcing gymnasts to work on certain skills is largely the reason why we still have compulsories at the international level. Most nations more developed in the sport are in favor of eliminating them, but others prefer to keep them since they cannot compete adequately with the best in optionals. Their gymnasts are usually still at the developmental levels and need the discipline and direction of compulsory routines.

Individual skills in the compulsories are not extraordinarily difficult, but often the combinations of the skills may be very difficult. The gymnast must perform with good technique to execute each skill to its maximum degree.

The best compulsories usually integrate very difficult combinations. Each skill requires nearly perfect execution of the skill immediately preceding it. Obviously, since compulsories represent 50% of the score, the gymnast will spend a lot of time working on them. The hope is that sheer repetition may aid learning and raise the general level of gymnastics by developing good technique.

Determining the direction of gymnastics is done through education in better technique and by forcing certain categories of skills into the compulsory. For example, after the streulli (a backward roll to a handstand from the upper arms) was included on the parallel bar compulsories, it was then seen more in the optional work.

In women's compulsories, when the handspring-full (in which the gymnast flips forward from feet to hands to feet) was used as the compulsory vault, this meant that no one could use the handspring-full in optional vaults. This led to an increase in vaulting skills as everyone turned to other categories for optional work. By including large swinging skills in the compulsory for all bar events, gymnasts have been forced to learn to swing better.

Age-group compulsories must be chosen carefully so that those who graduate from this program to become Elite gymnasts will have been through training regimes that will help them remain in contention at international levels.

The format for competition of compulsories is similar to that of optionals. The event order remains the same and the number of skills required are the same. However, it is usually forbidden to include C, or superior level, difficulty skills in the routine. What usually happens is that the best gymnasts make the compulsory skills appear to be C level simply by executing them better.

The compulsory routines are usually performed before the optionals. In the Olympics and World Championships, the compulsories are competed in the first two days by men and women, followed by individual all-around competition, and then individual event finals.

It is not uncommon to find athletes who have strengths and weaknesses in both the optional and compulsory portions of gymnastics. The winner is not decided by one score or the other, but by combined scores. Therefore, a gymnast weak in compulsories might make up for lost ground in the optional routines. However, the best athletes are usually very accomplished at both.

Compulsories may be coming to a close in the next Olympics. The level of gymnastics at present is so high at the international level that compulsories are becoming more of a nuisance than a help.

WHAT DO JUDGES DO?

Judges evaluate gymnasts in competition. They decide the winners, losers, places, ranks, champions, successes, and failures. This is a high-powered position and the judges usually do not take this responsibility lightly.

Judges must study the rules of the sport thoroughly to determine an accurate score for any given routine. They should begin by studying the Federation of International Gymnastics Code of Points. This code is a thick book containing most of the rules of the sport. There are a few additions and changing interpretations of the original code from time to time, but this book largely contains all of the information that judges need to know.

To become a judge, a person needs to apply to the state judging director, or regional judging director if there is not a state one. The judging organization for men is called the NGJA, or National Gymnastics Judging Association. For women, the organization is the NAWGJ or the National Association of Women's Gymnastics Judges. Each organization has a hierarchy of officials and committees for determining policies and procedures. A potential judge needs to apply to the organization for membership and then begins testing.

The testing of judges is complicated and thorough. They must undergo a testing and rating system far more difficult than any that currently goes on for coaches. Tests are offered periodically through the year at selected sites.

The judge must know all the various difficulties of skills in the A, B, and C format. He or she must know what mistakes get deductions. In other words, the judge must know that bending the legs receives an execution deduction, while a performance not having enough difficulty involved receives a difficulty deduction. The judge must apply all the deductions quickly, and completely without bias.

The judge should record on paper as much of the routine as possible by noting the difficulty of each skill, deductions for each skill, name of each skill, and any other special occurrences during a routine. The judge then must know and apply deductions that apply to the whole routine in general. For example, if the gymnast fails to perform a certain kind or category of skill, then the judge must levy the appropriate deduction. Of course, the judge does not know that the skill has been left out until the routine is over. The judge also must determine if the combination of any of the skills merits raising the difficulty evaluation. The judge then must add up the deductions, evaluate all the combination or composition requirements, and deduct the score from 10.00 to arrive at the score. These points are then submitted to the superior, or head, judge to be compared with all the other judges' scores. The judge usually has only about 20 seconds to finalize the evaluation.

When the score arrives at the head judge's table, he or she must determine if the scores are within range. This means that in a routine where the scores are above 9.0, the two middle scores must be a certain number of tenths apart. As the level of the routines (and thus the score) is lowered, the spread of the two middle scores can be a little wider. This control of the spread helps keep the scores proportionate with the final analysis.

The superior judge must apply these rules, plus any other special deductions above and beyond the simple evaluation of the performance. For example, in women's gymnastics, the out-of-bounds deductions for floor exercise are taken by the superior judge from the average score. The average score, or the score that actually counts, is the average of the two middle scores after the high score and the low score have been thrown out. If there are only two judges, both scores are averaged but the scores must still be within the range defined by the code of points for each level of scores.

At World Championships and Olympic Games, there are five judges. The fifth judge is actually the superior judge and makes all the special determinations. The other four judges produce the counting scores.

The superior judge can call the four judges together if the scores are not within the range defined by the code that's acceptable at each level. These occasions when the judges come together to discuss their evaluations of a particular exercise are called conferences, which are fairly short but are often a source of frustration for both competitor and spectator. The alternative is less well-judged competitions. These conferences can be very heated at times, especially in international competitions. The superior judge might try to force the opinions of the judges toward his or her way of thinking by intimidation and thereby influence the direction of the scoring and winners. If the judges can't agree then the superior judge can have his or her score averaged with the average score of the two middle judges' scores to arrive at a new score and it will become the counting score for the gymnast.

This means that the superior judge must assess every routine right along with all the other judges in an event. It also means that the superior judge can influence the score quite a bit by simply taking the option open by the rules to use his or her own score for averaging with the average score of the other four judges. This can bring the counting score of the gymnast up or down depending upon the value of the superior judge's score. If the superior judge's score is much higher than the average score of the four judges, then there can be quite a big change in the counting score.

Besides having to deal with rules, routines, performance evaluation, possible superior judge interference, keeping scores within a range of the rest of the panel, and watching the routine closely, the judge must also be able to deal with protests or inquiries.

The rules allow for a protest when the coach, team leader, or head of the delegation disagrees strongly with the score levied. The protest procedure (called inquiry in women's gymnastics) is set rather strictly. There is only a limited amount of time after the completion of the event rotation in which to file. The protest must be written in a certain format and delivered to the meet referee or head of the technical committee for the competition, sometimes only by a certain member of the offended delegation, and reasons for protests are limited. For example, you cannot protest because another gymnast repeated mistakes that your team's gymnast made and still received a higher score. The protest cannot be a comparative analysis of the scores. It must refer to specific occurrences in the routine of the gymnast in question and must always be made with the utmost respect. In other words, the protest cannot simply be a character assassination directed at the judges.

In women's gymnastics, you can inquire about the application of special deductions in the event of unusual occurrences such as someone yelling to the athlete, failure to remount in time after a fall, or whether the routine was over or under time. You can also inquire to make sure that the judges saw all the skills properly and knew that the combination in question might receive a higher difficulty evaluation.

The protest, or inquiry, procedure is not simply an opportunity to complain but must be directed to actual discrepancies in the application of the rules. There is no guarantee that the scores will be changed to reflect the nature of the protest. In fact, a good guess is that protests are honored less than half the time.

Being a judge can be a very interesting and rewarding job. United States judges accompany their teams overseas and represent their country as the American judge in foreign competitions. The ranking judges usually also act as the heads of delegations when U.S. teams go overseas. Judges must study hard but, of course, they get a stipend for their services when judging in the United States. The payment usually does not begin to cover the expenses incurred through purchasing the judging uniform, paying for study materials, attending the many required clinics, and sometimes for missing work. The judges in the United States are generally considered the most objective in the world, as well as the most knowledgeable about the rules, and most conscientious in their application.

Anyone interested in gymnastics who would like to become an active participant and influential contributor can look to judging as a possible means of enjoying a close relationship with gymnastics and helping many young people and the sport.

5

UNDERSTANDING SKILLS

The most important aspect of learning gymnastics skills is perfecting them so that subsequent skills may be performed with greater ease, height, power, and attractiveness.

The gymnast must learn hundreds and sometimes thousands of skills. Difficult skills may be used to earn a higher score. Some skills are considered basics because only the rankest beginners might do them. They do not add points but form the basis for the development of other skills, or might be part of the "unseen" part of performances. Unseen skills are those that allow the gymnast to get into support on an apparatus or begin a skill. The unseen skills are also those that the gymnast uses to recover from a fall, to conserve strength, to mount the equipment, and to develop strength and flexibility.

The selection and description of skills for a book of this nature is very difficult. Considering that there are thousands of them, their simple selection is always a controversy; you can never really know what everyone might be interested in seeing. Then, there is never enough space to show all the photos and cover all the nuances that may go into a skill.

Should we stick with the basics? There are hundreds of books that cover these skills. Should we cover only skills that meet composition requirements (i.e., those skills that meet the requirements for events)? There are too many of those, also. Should we use only the high-level skills that meet composition requirements? There are too many of those, also. Should we use only the high-level skills seen on television? These may give a slanted idea of the progressive nature of gymnastics.

So, where do we begin? After shooting over 150 rolls of film, we made our decision on which skills to describe. Some of the finest athletes in the Western Hemisphere have been photographed at the 1983 Championships of the USA, at the Mid-America Twisters training in Northbrook, in Colorado Springs Olympic Training Center, and at many other locations.

The major selection criteria were whether the skill was typical of the event and whether the photos could tell you something valuable about the event, demonstrate the universality of the technique, and enhance the beginner's ability to recognize nuances displayed in related skills. The gymnast must develop a sincere sense of duty in doing the basics thoroughly as well as pursuing high-level skills and difficult techniques.

WOMEN'S SKILLS

We will begin with the women's events. The women's events include skills slightly more fundamental than the men's. This is because there are a larger number of young female gymnasts at the lower beginning levels. The second section covering men's skills will include those skills showing some of our nation's best gymnasts.

Floor Exercise

The floor exercise event for women consists of tumbling and dance skills.

The tumbling moves included here are those that are important to floor exercise, and fundamental to good gymnastics. Dancing skills are more individual and photographs generally can't impart much helpful information.

The Aerial Cartwheel

The aerial cartwheel is one of the first airborne skills that the young female gymnast learns. It is also one of the few skills in the sport that the young gymnast often teaches herself. The aerial is important for floor exercise and balance beam (Fig. 11).

The aerial begins from a short run or from a stand. The gymnast in the photos has taken a short run and is in mid-hurdle (a preparation for positioning the feet properly) before placing her take-off leg on the mat and beginning the take-off process. The gymnast should take a rather low and long hurdle prior to the take-off. The gymnast will pass through a long lunge position as she places her take-off foot on the mat.

The gymnast lowers her torso close to the take-off leg during the approach. This lowering of the torso onto the take-off leg, which is the source of power for propulsion, is very important and is the portion of the skill most often neglected.

It is also important to understand the "rhythm" of the take-off. As the gymnast steps onto her take-off foot, she does not kick the rear leg right away. She must wait until her upper body is even closer to the mat before kicking her rear leg. This is the important difference between the aerial cartwheel and the regular cartwheel, in which hands are placed on the mat.

As the gymnast becomes airborne, you can see that she has completed a quarter-turn. Her legs are split and she can see the mat that she just left. She will next touch the mat with her landing leg. The gymnast who has trouble with the aerial cartwheel usually does not lower her chest close enough to the take-off leg, does not kick hard enough, kicks too soon, or runs too far. The successful aerial really travels only a very short distance.

The gymnast should practice this skill with sufficient matting and always perform it on a line so that its straightness at take-off can be maintained. This skill can later be transferred to the balance beam. The positioning of the arms is not too important as long as the gymnast is able to stay in a straight line.

Round-Off — Flip-Flop to Full Twist

This sequence contains three skills.

The first is very basic, the second high beginning, and the third intermediate in difficulty (Fig. 12). The round-off flip-flop to full twisting somersault is one of the most frequently used tumbling passes of the intermediate level gymnast. Since it contains skills absolutely vital to the performance of gymnastics, each skill will be explained in some detail.

The round-off usually begins from a run, and consists of a hurdle followed by the early movements of a cartwheel. The movements of the round-off are somewhat different from the cartwheel as the reach for the mat is considerably more forward and the turn is usually done quite a bit later. The gymnast should strive to cover as much distance on the round-off as possible by stepping long through the lunge and reaching extra far forward with the hands before placing them far apart on the mat with the fingers turned toward each other. The gymnast should have her elbows slightly bent so that she can push forcefully into the snap-down. The snap-down is the portion of the exercise in which the gymnast focuses built-up momentum for the flip by whipping her piked legs down and pushing forcefully from her hands to land on her feet. During the handstand portion of the round-off the legs should be nearly together and pivoted to the quarter-turn position.

The goal of the round-off is to turn around and thereby continue to tumble backward. The round-off should allow the gymnast to build more momentum in a horizontal direction from the run and hurdle. The longer the round-off,

11A

11B

11D

Fig. 11 *During the aerial cartwheel the gymnast starts her hurdle with one foot still on the mat.*

11C

12A   12B   12C

Fig. 12   *The round-off—flip-flop to full twist requires three skills, as demonstrated by this gymnast, and it should be long, low, and close to the ground. The length is determined by the horizontal speed.*

12G

12D

12E

12F

generally the more force produced. The only exception to this is the snap-down phase which follows the handstand. The snap-down should be quick and explosive so that the gymnast can use her legs again to promote the horizontal momentum as she arches backward into the flip-flop to follow.

The gymnast in the photos can be seen reaching forward during the hand placement of the round-off and pushing forcefully during the snap-down phase. The gymnast's typical mistakes during the round-off consist of not maintaining horizontal momentum by covering too great a distance during the round-off, or collapsing in a variety of different ways during the handstand portion.

The flip-flop that follows the round-off represents one of the major milestones for the young gymnast. Most young gymnasts consider themselves accomplished when they learn the flip-flop. However, it simply represents a step in the normal tumbling pass as the gymnast uses the flip-flop to continue to develop more force to be used during the somersault that follows.

The flip-flop should be long and low and very close to the ground. The length is controlled largely by the gymnast's horizontal momentum obtained during the round-off. The flip-flop is not really a dive to a handstand. It is more closely related to an airborne back-limber.

The gymnast should turn her hands in so that the fingers point toward each other during the hand support portion of the flip-flop. The gymnast's elbows will bend during the hand-support phase and, although it should not be encouraged to the point of collapse, this bending should allow the gymnast to have a more forceful push into the snap-down prior to the somersault.

Typical mistakes in the flip-flop include going too high so that the gymnast lands heavily on her hands, forcing her to arrest all the downward motion of the flip-flop to reconvert this into upward motion during the snap-down. The snap-down allows the gymnast to begin the upward motion of the torso into the take-off of the somersault.

The snap-down portion of the flip-flop is a much overlooked portion of the skill and should be very forceful and explosive to create the speed necessary to rise over the feet quickly.

The somersault begins the moment the feet contact the floor after the snap-down of the flip-flop. The gymnast can be seen during the take-off in the photo. Her arms are slightly forward of her body and she is extending her knees and hips to the maximum to allow her to get off the mat quickly and into the somersault. The efficiency of the take-off depends upon the speed of the gymnast's rising over her feet after the snap-down. This quickness is largely determined by the forcefulness of the push of the shoulders during the snap-down.

The somersault in this particular case includes one full twist about the long axis of the body. This is shown during the take-off as the gymnast turns

68

slightly as she finishes the take-off actions. The twist in most somersaults in gymnastics is performed by turning slightly from the supporting surface (in this case, the mat). It continues during the airborne phase in which the gymnast continues and finishes the amount of twist she wants to perform.

It is difficult for the gymnast to provide enough force to complete both the somersault and a turn or twist at the same time, so she must be very efficient during the round-off and flip-flop, which provide most of the force. Therefore, the gymnast should spend a great deal of time perfecting the power and efficiency of the entire sequence.

The full twist is performed by turning slightly during the take-off and then continuing this turn once airborne. In the full twist, the gymnast may lose orientation while somersaulting and twisting. The full twisting somersault should be approached carefully to avoid danger and injury.

The gymnastics coach usually spots or catches the gymnast during her first few executions of this skill, or she wears a spotting belt (a belt with ropes extending from the sides which the coach and an assistant grasp to keep the gymnast from falling). Or the gymnast will perform the skill into a foam pit, which is full of cushiony material to break her fall. It usually takes a few weeks for the gymnast to come to grips with turning in two orientations simultaneously. The average gymnast is quite capable of doing this with a little practice and usually the gymnast and coach can succeed at the full twist in a few weeks.

Round-Off — Flip-Flop to Double Twist

The double twist is a minimum requirement for floor exercise in women's gymnastics. As Bill Sands lectures on gymnastics around the country, the most frequent questions he is asked concerns the double twist. The double twist forms the major tumbling element for the lower levels and usually the dismount or second pass elements at the higher levels (Fig. 13).

The double twist begins with the round-off and flip-flop, as discussed earlier. The reader should note the positions of the gymnast in the photographs as she shows some of the most important positions. Note the distance between the hands in the round-off, length of the flip-flop from feet to hands, slight turn of the body at foot contact for take-off, and the relative stretch of the body during the twisting phases.

The arm action is usually of much interest in twisting skills and the reader can see that the arms of the gymnast during foot contact for the take-off are about eye-level and moving upward. The arms are quite rounded and held away from the body, indicative of a strong push from the mat during the snap-down. It is very important for the gymnast to use a wide arm position to initiate the twist and then to pull the arms in closer to her body as the twist accelerates.

Fig. 13 *The round-off—flip-flop to double twist requires considerable stretch of the body.*

13A

13B

13E

13F

13C

13D

13G

13H

It should be noted that the arm action is not responsible for the twist, but acts to conserve the turn created by the gymnast at take-off by twisting the body slightly from the mat. Actually, the arm action is much more important for establishing the somersault than for establishing the twist, but it is in fact the speed of the somersault and the snap-down that creates most of the forces that the gymnast will ultimately work with in the twist and the flip.

Russian Lift Front Somersault

Perhaps the simplest way to show a variety in your tumbling routines is to perform tumbling both backward and forward.

At this moment, forward tumbling is not prized as highly as backward tumbling and it is rather rare to see anyone doing forward tumbling skills except as connections to more backward tumbling. This is mostly due to the fact that backward tumbling is significantly easier to perform *well*. Forward tumbling is usually a little harder to learn due to orientation problems but, once learned, it can become as easy as backward tumbling for some athletes. The Russian lift front somersault is a common skill which the younger gymnast can perform safely without much previous experience (Fig. 14).

The Russian lift front somersault begins from a short run-up followed by a hurdle during which the gymnast brings both feet together so he or she can jump or "punch" off both feet for the take-off into the front somersault. The run must be quick and the gymnast should be discouraged from taking too many steps or running a long distance, because it makes the take-off more problematic.

During the hurdle the feet should travel low to the ground almost as if the gymnast were trying to slip her feet under the mat. The feet should land well in front of the body with knees slightly flexed and toes landing first. During this hurdle phase, the gymnast brings her arms from alternate swinging in the run to a position about chest high in front of her body. This position is called the "sleep walk" position.

As the feet are nearing the floor in the hurdle, the gymnast begins swinging her arms in a forward-to-downward and then upward-and-backward direction. This is somewhat like the butterfly stroke in swimming. The trick of the arm swing is to have the arms swinging upward and behind the body as the feet are pushing the mat downward. This arm action is very good for the front somersault because it nearly "pulls" the gymnast off the floor and into the somersault by the transfer of momentum of the swinging arms into the rest of the body.

As the gymnast performs the take-off, her body will pass over and slightly in front of her feet. The moment her body is positioned slightly over her feet, she will leave the ground and tuck.

14A   14B

Fig. 14   *The Russian lift front somersault is a common floor exercise maneuver. Note the arms during takeoff.*

14C   14D

The tuck in the front somersault should be quick and tight. The front somersault gains some of its difficulty in forcing the gymnast to perform a blind, or nearly blind, landing. This is because the gymnast's legs block her from seeing the floor early as the somersault completes itself. The gymnast should look farther forward for the floor instead of directly under her and she should be well schooled in keeping her knees slightly bent throughout the landing phases to prevent landing on straight legs, which would prevent her from cushioning the impact.

In the early learning stages, the gymnast should perform all of the somersaults into a pit or soft landing mat. This will help prevent accidents from miscalculations on landing and provide a soft area for the gymnast to land seated if she does not produce enough force at take-off.

The gymnast should also know how to perform a cowboy tuck. In this tuck, the hips and knees are bent but, instead of having the shins together, the knees and feet are very far apart. This tuck is slightly tighter than the traditional tuck and allows the gymnast to rotate faster. It also helps prevent some of the injuries that occur when the gymnast lands short and hits her nose on her knee. In the cowboy tuck, the knees are well out of the way of the face and the gymnast should easily avoid this type of injury.

Balance Beam

The balance beam skills are somewhat more difficult to select than the floor exercise skills since there is more variety in skills on the beam.

The gymnast may elect to perform widely varying types of skills which do not fit easily into any category. The complexity of balance beam skills has also gone from the difficult to the impossible.

One particular combination of one series of skills can be evaluated in many different ways, depending upon the order of skills, whether there is a stop or pause in the routine, what height the gymnast achieves on certain skills, or whether the gymnast lands on one foot or two. This makes the job of selecting important skills and categories of skills very difficult.

Whip-Up to Handstand

This skill was selected because it is relatively popular, does not require flight, and is performed while seated on the beam. Most of the skills in high-level balance beam work involve flight, are very high above the beam, very risky, and take years to learn. This skill, although not easy, can be learned by nearly everyone and still is one of the more beautiful skills in balance beam work (Fig. 15).

The gymnast begins in a straddled high V sit position facing the length of the beam. Her hands are between her legs in the so-called English position and her weight is on her seat. As the gymnast begins, she leans forward, bends her arms slightly and begins to swing her legs forward, downward, and up behind her. (A similar skill is used on the uneven bars.) The forward lean of the gymnast is crucial because it determines the direction that will follow. The gymnast must lean very far forward and take a rather nervous and close look at the balance beam.

The swing should be very forceful and the gymnast should try to keep her straddle narrow enough (i.e., her legs should be fairly close together) to facilitate the swing. If the gymnast starts out with a wide straddle, the swing will usually cause her feet to come together and strike the beam behind her. Ouch! The narrow straddle allows the legs to swing nearly parallel to the beam without striking anything. As the gymnast nears completion of the swing-up, her shoulders and head will move back over her hands and the lean forward will become much less pronounced. Finally, the gymnast arrives in a handstand. In these photos, the gymnast then splits her legs to arrive in an English handstand in split position.

The Flip-Flop

The flip-flop is usually one of the first airborne skills the gymnast learns on the balance beam (Fig. 16).

The flip-flop should be performed easily and confidently on the floor before ever attempting the skill on the balance beam. Once competence is achieved on the floor, the gymnast then must perform a few hundred flip-flops on a line on the floor to ensure symmetry. The gymnast should be capable of performing the flip-flop without collapsing in the shoulders and arms and without bending the legs or tucking the knees. After this is assured, the gymnast then can proceed to a balance beam that is low to the floor with soft mats all around and perhaps a stack of mats on either side of the beam placed so that the top surface is flush with the top edge of the balance beam. Then she may proceed to the low beam without mats and finally to the high beam.

The gymnast in the photos begins from a standing position with her arms at her sides. We recommend this rather than the usual sleep-walk position because the gymnast will become slightly off-balance backward if the arms swing backward in preparation for the jump instead of down and then backward. As can be seen in the photographs, after the initial "sit" phase before the jump, the gymnast is leaning well backward and off-balance. This position is difficult to learn because it is inherently scary to jump from positions that are out of balance and from which the gymnast cannot see where she is going. Thorough practice of the flip-flop on the floor using mat hills teaches the gym-

15A

15B

Fig. 15   *The whip-up to handstand has relatively minimal risk on the balance beam. The upward swing must be forceful with a narrow straddle.*

15D

15E

15C

15F

16A

16B

16E

Fig. 16   *The flip-flop on the beam requires that the gymnast perform in perfect symmetry. The key is the hand placement, which is practiced thousands of times on the ground before moving to the beam.*

nast to jump backward. As the ability to perform the jump backward increases, her confidence to perform the jump quickly enough to place her hands on the beam and still travel backward will be enhanced. Then, when it comes to the balance beam, the gymnast will already know how to make the flip-flop travel in the best direction.

The gymnast in the photo is performing the flip-flop step-out, or a flip-flop with a leg split in the handstand phase. This type of flip-flop is used presently in the compulsory exercises and we will most likely be seeing many more such flip-flops in the compulsories to come.

The gymnast in the photos is reaching rather far back for the hand placement. I would recommend against such a long hand placement as this tends to make the shoulders crooked during the handstand phase. Although the gymnast may not have too much trouble with the single flip-flop using this hand placement, she will later have lots of problems when she tries to connect two flip-flops in sequence because she will cover too much distance on the beam.

The ending position is the familiar lunge and should be well drilled and thoroughly experienced by all gymnasts, as its elegance and stability are hard to match.

Typical mistakes on the flip-flop include jumping without extending the knees completely, bending the arms at hand support, failure to push off the hands quickly during the step-down or snap-down, and failure to complete the lunge on landing.

Tuck-Back

The tuck-back somersault was first popularly introduced in 1972, when Olga Korbut performed the skill in the Munich Olympic Games. Gymnastics has not been the same since. Now, a tuck-back is nearly a requirement. At the least, the gymnast must show some type of somersault or flight phase skill (Fig. 17).

The tuck-back in the photo sequence is typical of most single tuck somersaults. The gymnast should follow the same precautions with the tuck-back as with the flip-flop in the previous section: the performance on the floor, then the line, then the low beam with mats stacked, then the low beam without mats stacked, and, finally, to the high balance beam.

The gymnast should attempt a fully extended jump, extending the knees and hips along with a forceful and quick swing of the arms. This will help establish plenty of altitude for the somersault with which the gymnast will complete the skill. Note that the gymnast in the photos sights the beam before she strikes it on landing.

The gymnast will land on the balance beam in a position a little bit like fourth position in ballet. That is, her feet will be turned out and separated

17A   17B   17C

Fig. 17   *The tuck-back requires the gymnast to jump with fully extended knees and hips with a forceful, quick swing of the arms.*

17D   17E

slightly on landing. The gymnast should attempt to land on the top of the beam in all tumbling skills. This means that the entire foot should be turned out, but it should not be reaching over the edge. The gymnast's foot should cover the entire top surface. Some of the European gymnasts often land on the arches of their feet. This seems to allow them to grip a little better, but we believe the injury potential of landing in this position is not worth the risk.

The gymnast adopts a special landing position upon impact to help guarantee her stability. This position is shown in the photos and should be well understood by the young gymnast. The body is contracted with the seat tucked under, weight between the feet, arms near the sides, and eyes focused on the beam. From this position, the gymnast regains her balance while low to the beam and then rises quickly to show the landing pose.

Aerial Walkover

The gymnast can achieve flight without taking off from both feet by using the aerial cartwheel discussed in the floor exercise section, or the aerial walkover discussed here (Fig. 18). The aerial walkover is actually easier to perform than the aerial cartwheel due to its greater symmetry. However, the aerial walkover is harder to learn since the gymnast generally cannot see the beam during the landing phase. The very flexible gymnast can sometimes see her foot hit the beam by arching and holding her head back during the latter phases of the skill.

Most rules that apply to the aerial cartwheel apply to the aerial walkover. The step prior to placing the take-off foot on the beam should be long. The gymnast probably should avoid a hurdle step since the hurdle gives her an opportunity to become crooked.

The kick should be very forceful and the same momentum requirements apply in the aerial walkover as in the aerial cartwheel. The kick comes rather late and the appearance of the skill should not resemble a front handspring. The rhythm has more of a "down-up" movement and not a "forward-kick" movement typical of the front handspring.

The kick has to be complete as shown by the airborne split position in the photos below. The forceful kick also helps the gymnast with landing since the inertia of the kick will help the gymnast rise back over her landing leg. The gymnast must arch a great deal on the aerial walkover. This is one of the few opportunities the gymnast has to arch a lot. Most of the time, we discourage a pronounced arch except in some high-level techniques and during some dance skills.

Typical errors on the aerial walkover include failure to lean the upper body forward enough, failure to kick completely, and turning in the second landing leg upon reaching the beam. This turning in of the second landing leg is one

18A   18B   18C

Fig. 18   *The aerial walkover on the beam requires a forceful kick like the one needed in an aerial cartwheel. The gymnast mustn't forget to turn in the second leg on landing.*

18D   18E   18F

of the most common reasons for falling and results in deductions on this skill. The gymnast is very likely to forget about the turn-out of the second leg while concentrating so intently on the landing foot reaching the beam safely.

Round-off Double Twist Dismount

No routine is complete without a dismount and this look at balance beam skills will end with a dismount that is one of the most common.

The round-off is a very important skill for modern gymnastics because it puts a tremendous amount of power at the disposal of the gymnast without her having to lose sight of the beam (Fig. 19). Round-offs are hard skills, though, because gymnasts have a difficult time making them straight enough to use on the balance beam. The nice thing about the round-off is that it is rated at a superior level of difficulty and therefore almost any dismount that you do after it is rated at an ever higher difficulty level due to the rules of combinations of skills.

The round-off is also one of those skills that even the very youngest of gymnasts can, and should, be working on. It does not require an inordinate amount of strength or flexibility and it allows the gymnast an early exposure to having to get both feet on the beam at the same time and "punching" from them for a subsequent somersault. In this series of photos, the round-off is part of the dismount, and the somersault does not have to land on the beam, thereby making it simpler to perform.

The photos show the gymnast about to place her hands on the beam. You should note that the distance between the arms is fairly wide and that the landing position on her feet is upright. Most young gymnasts land in a rather squatty position. This tendency results from the gymnast trying to expand her margin for error by slowing the snap-down. As the gymnast becomes more confident with the round-off, her ability to snap down quickly will improve.

The young gymnast can practice this skill by doing the round-off to the end of the floor balance beam and then a flip-flop or somersault onto a crash mat placed at the end of the beam and on the floor. This allows her a very large margin for error, as she will fall only a few inches if she makes a mistake and can still complete the skill safely. Therefore, although the skill is relatively difficult when viewed as a finished product, even the youngest gymnasts can work the skill early in their training on the low beam without danger.

The double twist is performed very much like the double twist referred to in floor exercise in which the body makes two revolutions. The actual type of somersault performed is not as important as the round-off which precedes the somersault. In fact, if the round-off is well executed you can pretty much take your pick of the type of somersault you want to perform.

Women's Vault

Handspring Vault

The handspring vault is one skill that has stood the test of time, and survived new technique crazes and any attempts to come up with an easy substitute in teaching competitors the intricacies of an event (Fig. 20). The handspring is the one single skill in gymnastics that you positively cannot get by without learning and perfecting, because it is the root, or essence, of nearly all vaults. The only exception that has developed recently is the sequence in which the gymnast does a round-off to the board, flip-flop to the horse, and then a snap-down and somersault after the horse. The round-off and flip-flop vaults do open a whole new world for vaulting, but most gymnasts must still rely on learning and perfecting the handspring before venturing into the more advanced and esoteric parts of vaulting.

The handspring should begin from a run-up of at least 66 feet. The run-up distance is largely at the discretion of the gymnast, but ideally should be longer than 66 feet. Research indicates that that is the distance required to reach 95% of your maximum running speed. However, the gymnast's maximum available run is about 77 feet. This means that the run must be very efficient. The gymnast should measure and mark her steps, always start on the same foot, always take the same number of steps, and always hurdle off the same foot.

The run can begin in a variety of movements largely dependent upon the personal preferences of the gymnast. As the gymnast moves down the runway, she should be constantly accelerating. If the gymnast spends her acceleration too soon, then she will generally slow down as she approaches the board and will perform a poor take-off and vault.

As the gymnast nears the board as shown in the first of the photos, she will prepare her arms for the hurdle. The hurdle serves to place the gymnast's feet together at the board and prepare her arms to receive the horse. The arms and legs are swinging alternately during the run and the hurdle prepares them to come together. The arm preparation actually occurs in the last half of the last step before the hurdle. The hurdle should be very low and very fast, and should resemble a running stride in its dimensions and dynamics. A hurdle that rises to afford more time to get the feet together, or prepare the arms, will only slow down the gymnast and cause her to descend onto the board, thus wasting force.

Upon arrival on the board, the gymnast will begin the take-off actions. She should have her seat tucked under at board contact to avoid arching or sagging in the middle body during take-off and losing force. The arms are swung quickly to a position ready to receive the horse and the legs extend explosively, using the springiness of the board to propel the gymnast to a handstand on top of the horse.

19A

19B

Fig. 19 *The somersault used in the round-off double twist dismount isn't as important as the preceding round-off, which is considered high-difficulty by judges. The landing on the beam before the somersault should be in an upright position.*

19E

19F

19C

19D

19G

87

20A

20B

Fig. 20 *The flight after contact with the horse on the handspring vault needs to be as high and far as possible. The knees should be slightly bent during the landing and the arms held overhead.*

20E

20C

20D

20F

20G

The preflight is the part of the vault between the take-off and contact with the horse. The preflight of the handspring should be just high enough for the gymnast to get to the horse fully extended and just low enough to prevent her from contacting the horse while descending onto it. At horse contact, the gymnast should be extremely extended with all body parts in perfect alignment.

As the gymnast learns other more difficult vaults, she might adapt the preflight and on-horse position. But, for the handspring alone, the body should be ramrod straight. The gymnast can enhance her push off the horse by explosively elevating the shoulders upon contact, and "punching" from the shoulder girdle.

The postflight is that portion of the vault between the horse contact and the landing on the mat. The postflight is usually the business part of the vault. It should be as high and far from the horse as possible since this is usually where the somersaulting and twisting will occur in more advanced skills. Therefore, the higher and farther the postflight, the more room and potential for displaying the somersault and/or twist safely and consistently.

The final phase of the handspring as shown in the photos can provide the gymnast with some excellent training in the landing of forward somersaulting and forward vaults. The gymnast should always keep her knees slightly bent during the landing and her arms overhead so that the arms do not fall and their inertia carry the gymnast forward.

Handspring Front Vault

The gymnast must run very fast and be very efficient and precise to perform vaults with somersaults such as the handspring front vault (Fig. 21). The gymnast in the photos shows a significant arch in the preflight, using her body position to provide a more explosive push to the horse, thereby bringing more force to the somersault and height to the postflight. The arch allows the gymnast to push off the horse by making her body into a sort of leaf spring. The leaf spring effect is called a "thorax thrust" by some authors, but it simply means that the gymnast uses an arch and then straightens the body out to push the horse harder during the support phase.

The description of the vault is rather obvious and can be left to the photos. The reader should note that the gymnast here is using the "cowboy tuck" mentioned in the Russian lift front somersault. The gymnast here is not accustomed to performing outside, good for pictures but unnerving to gymnasts, and so she uses the cowboy tuck for safety reasons.

Landing in the handspring front is very difficult. Often, the gymnast will land on her seat because of inadequacies in the handspring actions. The gymnast must also land without being able to see the mat directly under her. The landing can be improved by constant repetitions in which the gymnast spots her landing by looking for the floor farther forward rather than directly underneath herself.

Tsukahara Vault

The Tsukahara vault was first done by an American gymnast and was first called an O'Shaw, but Mitsuo Tsukahara of Japan was the first to do it in World or Olympic competition and therefore his name is attached to it (Fig. 22).

The Tsukahara is really a very easy vault to do, but very difficult to do well. It is one of the most common vaults performed and provides an easy start for other more difficult vaults. Twisting the Tsukahara, or using different body positions, is relatively simple to understand, although not simple to perform.

The Tsukahara begins from a run, hurdle, and take-off much like the handspring and the handspring front. The hurdle may have a little turn to facilitate the take-off which must be performed with a one-quarter, three-eighths, or one-half turn. The one-quarter and three-eighths turns seem to be the most efficient. The turn is initiated by twisting the body just after the legs hit the board and continuing this movement during the preflight phase. The gymnast must remain stretched during this turn as any collapse of the body during support can spell disaster for the postflight somersault. The legs should not be separated as the gymnast has done in the photos.

Upon hand contact with the horse, the gymnast will have performed a one-quarter to a three-eighths turn. The body should be stretched and arched sideways as well as in the back. The hands will contact the horse one at a time. The first hand provides the guidance and early support that will develop the support of the second hand and provide a sufficient foundation for the second hand to push forcefully into the snap-down.

The gymnast should begin to push off and assume the pike position before her body reaches the vertical position and should complete these actions at the vertical, at which point she should leave the horse and finish the somersault during the postflight.

The Tsukahara pictured here is done in pike position. All Tsukaharas begin as piked Tsukaharas. After the pike action during the push from the support phase, the gymnast can then do whatever she chooses provided she has enough force. She can twist, stretch the body out into the layout position, pike more tightly, tuck, etc.

Women's Uneven Bars

The uneven bars is perhaps the one event that has shown more progress than any other. The sequences, techniques, difficulty, and risk have evolved so far that the evaluation of the event has become very difficult. The performance of the event has also become more difficult.

The gymnast must learn to swing like a monkey, have the daring of a cat burglar, and the reckless abandon of a stunt woman. The most often-needed skills are the major releases in which the gymnast lets go of the bar, somer-

21A

21B

Fig. 21 *In the handspring front vault, the gymnast has to land without being able to see the mat below.*

21E

21C

21D

21F

93

22A   22B   22C

Fig. 22 *The turn in the piked Tsukahara vault is generated by twisting the body against the legs on the board and then continuing the movement during preflight.*

22D   22E   22F

saults, and recatches the bar again without losing swing or pausing in execution.

The uneven bars event is beautiful largely because of its engineering of sequences, not simply because of the elegance of the positions that the gymnast uses. This is important to understand since some skills are designed to bring a sigh due to their complexity and not simply for their beautiful positions. Uneven bars provide the same kind of thrills that we see in men's horizontal bar and the circus trapeze.

Free Hip Circle

The free hip circle is one of the first swinging skills that the gymnast learns, and is absolutely vital to the gymnast as a step in her learning about swing (Fig. 23). Every gymnast must learn how to do one at one time or another even though she may never actually use it in her competitive exercise. The free hip circle also forms an integral part of most compulsory exercises.

The free hip circle is also called a clear hip circle in FIG terminology. The free hip begins from a cast, in which the body is held in a rigidly-maintained position that is maintained as the gymnast moves up. The gymnast then moves the body backward by pushing forward with her hands and arriving in a position with her shoulders directly above the bar. The body position should be somewhat curved, hollow, or contracted. This is shown in the first photo.

The cast is critical to the ultimate success or failure of the performance of the free hip circle. The cast will "set up" her downswing so that the gymnast is able to circle the bar more efficiently and is more likely to circle at a distance from the bar that will allow her to move away and back to the handstand without loss of swing.

The downswing is begun by leaning backward even farther from the shoulders, and piking, or contracting, more dramatically. The pike reaches about 90 degrees when the shoulders are directly under the bar and the gymnast then begins to pull downward on the bar to raise the body, move it away from the bar, and return to the handstand.

The gymnast should be careful not to bend her arms on the downswing, pike before she descends below the bar, or pull in or bend her arms on the upswing. The gymnast should be strong enough to cast to a handstand before pursuing the free hip circle with any serious hope of executing one. The gymnast should also have enough strength to keep her body close enough to the bar during the circle to prevent centrifugal force and gravity from pulling her away from it.

Finally, the gymnast should pay particularly close attention to what her hands are doing as she circles the bar: a great deal can thus be learned about the nature of the swing. If the gymnast has difficulty moving her hands at all,

Fig. 23 *The important downswing in the free hip circle is begun by leaning far backward from the shoulders and contracting the body. The gymnast must be careful not to bend her arms during the downswing or upswing.*

23A

23D 23E

23B 23C
23F

97

it is because her elbows are bent. If the gymnast manages to move her hands all the way around the bar but has to change her grip at the end to give her support, then the gymnast may need to lean back more during the cast to obtain more swing.

The Stalder

The Stalder is named after Joseph Stalder, who was the first to perform the skill on the horizontal bar.

The Stalder today is one of the landmark skills that demonstrate higher levels of swing technique and of uneven bar composition than that of free hip circles (Fig. 24). The Stalder is rated as a superior, or C, level difficulty skill and is one of the best skills that a gymnast can learn for uneven bars. If the gymnast performs the skill well, it is very difficult to fall. The Stalder is easy to make consistent and it is rated high in difficulty. You can't ask for a better combination of qualities.

The skill does require a relatively sophisticated bar worker, but this move is definitely within the reach of most uneven bar gymnasts. The gymnast with longer arms and legs who possesses the ability to contract well in the chest and stomach will probably be successful in this skill.

The gymnast generally begins the Stalder in a handstand. The handstand is as important to the Stalder as the cast is to the free hip. The cast should be to a slightly under-balanced handstand. The gymnast who casts to a handstand that is balanced on top of the bar generally has a harder time getting far enough away from the bar on the downswing to realize enough swing to complete the circle. Therefore, the gymnast should cast to a seven-eighths handstand, not a whole one. This allows her to swing down before she starts the process of turning over or straddling her legs into the Stalder position at the bottom of the swing.

The gymnast in the photographs can be seen lowering her body and legs well behind the bar as she performs the downswing. This is important because a lot of swing helps the gymnast get her legs into the Stalder position. The downswing position shown in the photos helps the gymnast turn over quickly because she can use her legs as heavy weights to swing around her hips. This also helps the gymnast keep her seat close enough to the bar to facilitate the completion of the circle.

During the upswing the gymnast moves out of the pike position slightly and rides the swing high enough to change grip and place her wrists on top of the bar. The gymnast should try to keep her straddle narrow going into the Stalder and wide coming out. This helps the gymnast into and out of the tight inverted straddle position quickly. This can be seen quite clearly in the photos.

The reason that the Stalder is easy to perform consistently is that the gymnast who makes a mistake in the downswing, or simply lacks the swing to go explosively to the handstand on the upswing, can hold herself in the straddle pike position during the upswing until she has arrived on top of the bar. Then, she simply puts her legs together. This gives the gymnast a huge margin for error.

Giant Swing

The giant swing is a new addition to uneven bars, having come into fashion since 1978 (Fig. 25).

This skill has made the uneven bars more and more like the men's horizontal bar. The low bar has been the only deterrent to expanding the swing more and more. The smaller gymnast usually has an advantage on giant swings because she can swing farther from the high bar in the downswing than a taller one. However, most gymnasts are easily capable of doing a giant swing if they spread the bars all the way out. This means that the bars must be set at maximum width and the routine will be unlikely to contain any skills that stomach whip the low bar. This has caused a few problems in uneven bar work since the use of a giant swing sometimes forces the gymnast to avoid some of the fancier releases that result from stomach whipping the low bar. In contrast, the gymnast who whips the low bar may have some troubles doing giant swings. The fortunate ones are able to do both.

The giant swing, as shown in the photos, shows some of the same downswing requirements as the Stalder. The gymnast should begin in a seven-eighths handstand. She should swing well out over the low bar to get as much downswing momentum as possible. The only problem comes when she must clear the low bar. This is done by piking and straddling only enough to miss the bar without impairing the size of the swing. This usually means that the gymnast will nearly touch her legs and seat to the bar, missing by only an inch or so.

The gymnast passes the low bar with little room to spare and then must extend her body quickly to counteract the forces of gravity and her own downswing. The earlier the extension passing the low bar, the better the gymnast can make the transition from swinging down to swinging up. The upswing is initiated by lifting the legs upward forcefully from the hip and stomach and pulling down on the bar slightly with the arms. The explosive leg lift and arm pull usually aid the upswing forces as does shortening the upswing radius by piking and contracting in the stomach. The upswing raises the gymnast high enough to allow her to change her grip from a hanging position to a support position and then the giant swing is completed.

The typical mistakes of the young gymnast in the downswing are those propagated by hitting the low bar. The gymnast usually pikes and straddles earlier than she needs to and cuts out some precious downswing momentum that will later provide her with the force necessary to return to the top of the

24A

24B

Fig. 24   *In the Stalder on the uneven bars, a strong downswing helps the gymnast turn over quickly. The upswing consists of coming out of the pike position and riding the swing high enough to change grips.*

24E

24F

24C

24D

24G

24H

Fig. 25 *The giant swing, a relatively new skill, is gaining popularity in women's competition. It begins with a seven-eighths handstand.*

25A

25D

25B

25C

25E

25F

high bar. The young gymnast usually fails to extend quickly enough upon passing the low bar. The failure to extend quickly while passing the low bar results in the gymnast passing through the bottom of the swing piked. This pike is usually "ripped" out of position by gravity and forces an arched upswing through the inertia of the legs which are then moving backward. This arch is one of the prime enemies of the upswing and will quickly squelch any attempts to get back on top of the high bar.

The last mistake usually consists of arching or attempting the change grip much too early on the upswing, thereby lengthening the upswing radius too much and failing to achieve support through loss of speed.

Deltchev

The Deltchev represents the current trend on uneven bars. This move is named after Stoyan Deltchev, a Bulgarian who first performed the skill on the horizontal bar (Fig. 26). The particular Deltchev pictured here might well be called a Filatova since its crossed-grip downswing was first done by Maria Filatova of the Soviet Union. The skill consists of a giant downswing followed by a half turn and a front somersault to regrasp the high bar. Although somersaulting and regrasping the bar have been around for a while, this combination has not been so widespread and done from such varying positions as it has since 1978.

The gymnast begins as in a giant swing, but moves one hand to an overgrip position across the other hand. Therefore, this position is called a cross grip. This downswing grip helps turn the gymnast through the half-turn prior to the upswing by the very unwinding of the arms as shown in the photos of the upswing and release.

The downswing here is shown with legs together. Although the downswing can be done with a straddle, it is more difficult to keep the body in a straight line. The upswing consists of turning about the long axis of the body and then somersaulting to catch the bar between the legs. This somersault starts and finishes on the same bar and represents one of the most daring of the uneven bar skills.

The gymnast who seeks to perform skills like the Deltchev should be extraordinarily well-conditioned and already able to perform a giant swing easily along with other forms of somersaulting skills.

Double Flyaway

Continuing on the same idea as the Deltchev, the double flyaway dismount has been included due to its newly gained popularity, its development from men's horizontal bar, and its representation of things to come in uneven bars (Fig. 27).

The double flyaway consists of a giant downswing followed by a release on the upswing and two somersaults performed before landing.

The double flyaway obeys the same technique rules as the giant swing does for clearing the low bar and for passing through the bottom of the swing. The gymnast tucks during the upswing just prior to release. The somersault is performed using the force created by the giant swing and conserved in the tuck position.

Most of the problems in this dismount come from releasing too early or too late. These are also the result of failure to pass through the bottom of the swing in the proper position. If she passes the bottom correctly, the gymnast will be able to lift her legs quite easily and properly to aid the feeling of the upswing and to use her natural ability to release the bar at the appropriate moment. The gymnast who pulls into the bar and, perhaps, comes dangerously close to the high bar is usually using bent arms in the downswing or arching her back and piking her hips as she passes the bottom.

Analyzing the problems of the double flyaway are difficult. And like most other skills, it is best to pay close attention to detail long and dutifully, to avoid such problems rather than correct them once they have appeared.

MEN'S SKILLS

The men's skills are divided among six events. The photos were taken with the goal of providing a look at some of the top performers in the United States today. Among those pictured are Bart Conner, Jim Hartung, Mario McCutchen, Mitch Gaylord, and Phil Cahoy. These young men have been performing on the men's national team for many years and along with the others pictured, provide some of the best gymnastics America has ever seen.

Floor Exercise

The floor exercise for men usually consists of four tumbling passes, a press, another balance skill, some fancy corner movement and a few miscellaneous moves. The way that the gymnast fulfills this template, however, is limitless in its variety. First we'll discuss some of the more straightforward, simpler skills before moving on to the tumbling.

Fig. 26 *The Deltchev, a popular skill, begins with a cross-gripped giant downswing, half-turn, and front somersault.*

26A

26D

26E

26B

26C

26F

26G

27A

27E

Fig. 27 *The double flyaway is a giant downswing followed by a release on the upswing and two somersaults before landing.*

27B

27F

27C

27D

27G

27H

Flexibility and Balance

Flexibility must be shown by both men and women in gymnastics. With women, we have come to view the quality as almost commonplace, but with men it is a little more startling to see just how flexible the men can be and still remain so powerful. Figures 28, 29, 30, and 31 show the types of flexibility skills the men perform.

Balance is usually shown in the handstand positions. The reader can see balance, strength, and flexibility shown at the same time in one skill.

Tumbling

The tumbling in men's gymnastics is quite a sight for spectators. The men, with more strength and power than the women, are capable of tumbling so high and with such ease that they can be sheer pleasure to watch. The tumbling skills included here are typical of our top men gymnasts.

Double Back Pike Somersault

The double back pike somersault shown (Fig. 32) includes the round-off and flip-flop to demonstrate the relative similarities between the men and women performing the same skills. The gymnast performing the double pike is doing so during the warm-ups and landing onto a 4-inch landing mat for safety. This mat cannot be used during competition. The reader should note the stretch of the body during take-off and the tightness of the pike throughout the two somersaults. The round-off and flip-flop must be very efficient for the men as well as the women. Even though the men are stronger as a group then the women, they must move slightly heavier bodies; simply being strong is not enough to realize success.

Of course, it is relatively simple to watch the experienced and competent gymnast perform the skills and believe that the skills are quite easy. But the young gymnast learning and perfecting these types of skills should train them in protective foam pits, with competent and experienced spotters, and with the utmost respect for the risk and difficulty inherent in skills that require multiple somersaults. The learning time for a double somersault is usually between six to nine months after the layout is strong enough.

Full-In-Back-Out

The full-in-back-out, or just full-in, is a double somersault backward with a full twist in the first somersault thrown in for good measure (Fig. 33).

Fig. 28   *Jim Hartung shows his flexibility with a side split.*

Fig. 29   *Tim Daggett demonstrates the straddle "L" position.*

Fig. 30   *Tim Daggett in a wide-arm handstand.*

Fig. 31   *Jim Hartung demonstrates a strength skill with this planche.*

The full-in is usually done on the first pass of tumbling, but some of the best gymnasts now use the full-in for a pass later in the routine. The round-off and flip-flop have already been discussed, so we will take over here at the snap-down and the take-off for the full-in.

The photos show the gymnast during the snap-down and then just entering the twisting portion of the full twist in the first somersault. The complete and explosive stretch of the body is very important for the full-in take-off and thus the second photo in the sequence is of particular importance in our understanding of the skills. The third photo shows how high the gymnast has gone to be able to complete such a difficult skill, indicative of his innate power and efficiency in the round-off and the flip-flop.

The reader can also get an appreciation for how very fast you fall during a skill. The gymnast in the fourth photo is entering the second somersault and then in ⅙ of a second in the next photo has fallen to the floor with less than ¾ of a somersault.

Women gymnasts are doing the full-in-back-out much more now than ever before and enjoy the same technical requirements as the men. The gymnast should be able to perform the double somersault and a double twisting somersault with ease and confidence before attempting the full-in. As an idea of how difficult the full-in really is, let's say that the full-in is to a double-back somersault what a triple twist is to a layout. Although the gymnast might think that the double-back is a good enough foundation for attempting full-ins, the double somersault should be exemplary and not simply adequate.

Triple Twisting Somersault

After the gymnast is capable of twisting the somersault in tumbling, the race begins to see how many twists he or she can perform in one somersault. The count at the moment is stuck at three.

The triple twist (Fig. 34) is a good high-level skill for the young gymnast to learn since, although it is very, very, difficult, the gymnast who makes an error does not face as severe consequences as the gymnast performing the types of skills already mentioned. The athlete doing a triple twist who might make an error usually lands a little sideward, but almost always on his feet. The gymnast who makes a mistake on the double somersault may not land on his feet and the landings can be very uncomfortable.

Triple twists are very complex movements, and most male gymnasts shy away from this skill because it is, frankly, easier to perform a double somersault. The triple twist pictured here is performed by Jim Hartung and begins at the snap-down portion of the tumbling pass. The snap-down for the triple twist and the subsequent take-off differs somewhat from the double somersault, as the gymnast is attempting to get much more height during the triple twist than during the double somersaults.

32A

32B

Fig. 32   *A well-done double back pike somersault includes great stretch of the body upon takeoff and tightness of the pike throughout the somersaults.*

32E

32F

32G

32C

32D

32H

32I

33A   33B

Fig. 33 *These photos show the gymnast at these stages of the full-in back-out move: During snapdown, entering the twist, peak of the maneuver, and entering the final somersault.*

33C

33D

33E

34A

34B

34D

Fig. 34 *Skillful gymnasts, such as Jim Hartung, are up to three twists in the floor exercise, and this sequence shows him at a variety of stages in each twist.*

34C

34E

The main goal of the take-off during the triple twist is to achieve enough height so that the gymnast will have enough time to complete all three revolutions before striking the mat again. It may seem to be a huge task, when we consider that the gymnast may somersault so fast that his feet hit the mat before he has enough time to turn around three times. Therefore, the name of the game in the triple is altitude. The name of the game in double somersaults is the somersault.

The reader should note that the gymnast is particularly stretched during the take-off phase. The body remains stretched throughout the twisting portions of the skill to facilitate the speed of the twist and the gymnast must remain very rigid during the somersault so that the twisting forces are not lost through the general floppiness of the body position.

Pommel Horse

The pommel horse consists of two types of swing: scissor, or pendular, swings, and circular, or flank, circle swings. We might be able to add a few new types of swings lately as the gymnasts are now dismounting through handstands and the "spindle" swing is a combination of circling in one direction and twisting the body around its long axis in the other direction.

The pommel horse offers only a few different ways of moving about it. Unfortunately, that is where the simplicity ends. The very intricacy of the movements on the pommel horse and the infinite combinations that the gymnast can perform by putting the skills together makes the pommel horse one of the more esoteric events. In fact, often only the very experienced coach and gymnast can recite the names of the skills as quickly as the gymnast is performing them without falling behind and getting lost. The pommel horse, for all its complexity, has evolved through only a few major changes—most of them recent.

Scissors

The scissor swing is the type learned first by most young gymnasts.

The scissors (Fig. 35) are done in two directions, forward or backward, depending upon which part of the body is leading during the swing. If the front side of the body is leading, it is called a front scissor. If the back side of the body is leading . . . back scissor.

The gymnast must perform both types of scissors in his routine, but he need only do one type more than once in succession. The front scissors are almost always chosen as the one that the gymnast repeats a few times since it is much easier to lift the legs high in the front scissor. The back scissor is limited by

35A

35B

Fig. 35 *A scissor on the pommel horse can be forward, when the front of the body leads, or backward, when the back side leads.*

35C

35D

the flexibility of the hip in getting the leg high. To do so, the gymnast must swing very high, which is considerably more difficult than just lifting the leg up.

At this time, the scissor family of skills has been considerably elevated in difficulty by gymnasts performing turns during the scissor and combining them with the "Thomas Flair," inaugurated by American gymnast Kurt Thomas.

The scissor shown here is a forward scissor and one can see that the name comes from the actions of the legs as they knife up and down beside the horse. You can get an appreciation for this type of swing by looking at the clearance above the horse obtained at the peak of the swings. Scissors are also among the most beautiful and easily recognized of the skills on the pommel horse.

The gymnast performing the scissors should turn his torso considerably to avoid hitting the horse with his legs. The scissor action should turn the hips enough to allow as much distance from the sides of the horse as possible. Touching the horse or brushing the horse with the legs brings deductions.

The competitor must continually move his body during all pommel horse skills. This means that there is a considerable weight shift during the scissor, as can be seen by the lean of the gymnast over his supporting arm.

Russian to Back Moore Down

This skill demonstrates good swing technique, which is what pommel horse is all about (Fig. 36).

The gymnast is shown performing the latter part of a Russian Moore, in which he pivots around both pommels without flanking over the horse, but facing it at all times. After the Russian Moore, the gymnast performs a Back Moore, one of the more prevalent types of skills now performed on the modern pommel horse. The Back Moore as the pictures show, is a skill in which the athlete must perform circling movements with both hands either on one pommel or behind his back. This type of swing is especially difficult, yet it is what makes the pommel horse the exciting and extraordinarily difficult event that it is.

It should be obvious that the circular swing technique of the gymnast who endeavors to accomplish such skills should be very well developed. This is partially due to the fact that the gymnast must swing in a fairly high plane for there to be enough room to place his hands behind his back, and continue to swing without sitting on the hands.

The reader should note the height of the swing of the gymnast's legs, the amount of lean of the upper body to promote the ability to swing in such a fashion, and the pushed-downward position of each shoulder. The young gymnast usually fails to swing in a high plane, and lean the body in the appropriate direction at the appropriate time. Because of lack of strength, he often sags badly in the shoulder girdle. It is the ability of the gymnast to push completely through the shoulders that affords some of the clearance from the horse necessay to perform the circular swing with such height.

Still Rings

The still rings is perhaps the most stubborn event for showing progress. The skills on the rings are still much the way they were ten years ago. Although there are more twists in dismounts and perhaps an extra somersault, most of the skills that make up the body of the routine are still very similar. However, the gymnast's techniques have improved markedly, swings are done more freely with straighter arms, and we have attained a nice balance between swing and strength. It is in the strength moves that some significant changes have occurred, since we now see a wider variety of related skills which are not all the traditional "cross."

The event is called the still rings because the rings should be still for most of the routine. This is a little deceptive. When you watch a ring routine, the rings are often far from being still. The "still" part of the still rings means that when the gymnast wants to be still, he is, e.g., when he is holding a pose.

The still positions are the most easily understood and recognizable. The gymnast should blend swing and stillness or balance and strength. These positions often show strength by virtue of the gymnast's ability to support himself in an unlikely pose. There are other strength skills that include slow movements up and down, to and from handstands. The skills included here show a variety of common movements and hold parts.

Hold Parts

Skills in which the gymnast should be still are shown here. The first is the handstand. The handstand itself does not seem particularly difficult to perform when you think of the handstands on other events. On the still rings, this is quite another story (Fig. 37).

The rings are free to move, so that not only does the gymnast have to hold his body upright and support the position, he must also keep the rings from moving around. This is like trying to balance a handstand on a chair, tilting on one leg on an icy surface. A handstand on the still rings is far more difficult than handstands anywhere else in the sport. The strength necessary simply to keep the rings in one place is extraordinary. The gymnast should attempt to keep the rings under control by turning the forward parts of the rings outward and away from each other and maintaining the rest of the body in a very still and rigid position.

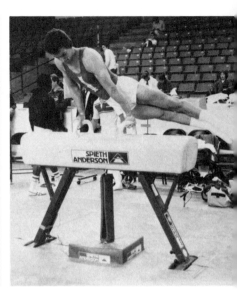

36A
36B
36C

Fig. 36   Phil Cahoy is performing the late stages of a Russian to back Moore, a pivot around both pommels without flanking over the horse.

36G

36H

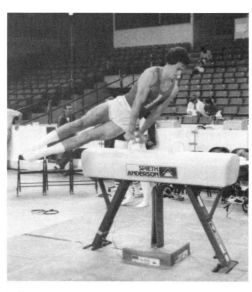

36D

36E

36F

36I

36J

36K

Fig. 37   *A handstand on the rings.*

Fig. 38 *The back lever is one of the first skills a gymnast learns on the rings.*

Back Lever

The back lever is usually the first strength pose skill that the young gymnast learns (Fig. 38). Much of the difficulty of the skill is self-evident in this photo. The gymnast has an easier time with this skill than with some of the other strength skills because the anatomy of the shoulder helps him hold the position, whereas he enjoys no such advantage in other moves. The gymnast should be aware that the skill is not easy. It's just easier than some of the other strength skills that he might try to learn on the rings.

The gymnast should be especially aware of his elbows on the rings since a great deal of stress in some of the strength poses is directed to them. Caution and care need to be exercised in training and learning to avoid undue stress to the tender tissues in the elbows and to avoid damaging them beyond their daily recuperation rate.

Fig. 39 *The Planche on the rings requires considerable strength.*

Planche

The Planche is a skill that has been around for many years, yet it is still exciting to see a gymnast actually support himself in such a fashion (Fig. 39). There is not much to be said for learning a Planche other than that the gymnast had better be awfully strong.

Giant Swing

The first of the swing skills we'll cover is the giant swing (Fig. 40). This skill covers getting down from the handstand and up from the bottom of the swing.

The gymnast pictured here is showing exemplary technique. He pushes the rings almost directly forward as he begins the downswing. The gymnasts doing giant swings in the past generally pushed the rings sideward to slow the descent before pushing them forward and this kept the swing slower and more easily under control.

As the swing techniques have progressed, this newer technique of pushing the rings directly forward gives the gymnast significantly more swing to perform skills during the upswing using superior positions such as the straight arms demonstrated by the athlete pictured here.

The gymnast performs the downswing in an arched position so that his body hits the bottom of the arc in a consecutive fashion starting with his shoulders, then torso, then hips, and finally legs, which allows him to spread the shock over a greater distance and thereby lessen the impact. The gymnast also uses this arch to delay his legs through the bottom of the swing and afford them a shipping action that snaps them upward into the upswing with great force and seemingly little muscular effort. This explosive upswing allows the gymnast to perform release skills higher and faster and allows superior positioning of the body.

The reader should also note that the gymnast spreads the rings outward during the upswing, which effectively shortens the upswing radius promoting the rise and allows the gymnast to delay using his arms to pull him upward until he is closer to the handstand position.

This newer and more reckless swing movement is indicative of the more advanced techniques being demonstrated by modern gymnasts. The gymnasts now wear a more specialized grip for such swings including a dowel made of wood or plastic that acts like a claw to keep the gymnast attached to the rings after he swings down and allows him to release during the dismount. The gymnast without such hand grips is at a very distinct safety disadvantage.

Half In - Half Out Dismount

The rings is a peculiar event in that the gymnast does not let go of the rings until the dismount, unlike in other events, where releases and regrasps are an integral part of the routine. This and the ability to swing down from a handstand give the gymnast the opportunity to do some rather complex dismounts.

The compulsory dismount on the rings is the half in - half out dismount, which consists of a half twist in the first somersault followed by a half twist in the second somersault (Fig. 41). This dismount is also used in optional exercises.

Fig. 40 *The new technique of pushing the rings forward during the giant swing gives the gymnast more swing. The downswing is performed in an arched position, which allows the body to hit the bottom in sequence.*

40A

40D 40E

Fig. 41 *The half-in half-out dismount on the rings is a very popular dismount. Here it is being performed with a layout body position.*

41A

41D 41E

41B   41C

41F   41G

The half in - half out is performed by most gymnasts as their dismount. The person pictured here is performing the dismount with a layout body position unlike the tuck position used by most other gymnasts. The dismount begins from a downswing from the handstand that obeys most of the same rules as the giant swing listed previously. The upswing is then marked by an abrupt pull and release at a position above the rings themselves. The pull is a little non-symmetrical to initiate the twist. The gymnast then performs the first half-twist with the first somersault and the second half-twist during the second somersault.

The reason for the popularity of the half in - half out somersault is that the gymnast can see the mat through almost all of the entire skill, allowing him to make a secure landing. The tuck position, used by most gymnasts, allows them to rotate more quickly than the layout and, therefore, more safely. The tuck is not a great deterrent to twists of the half-turn variety and is therefore a very nice dismount for the gymnast.

Vaulting

As discussed earlier, men's vaulting is different in many respects from women's vaulting. First, the male gymnast has to vault over the length of the horse. Second, the horse is higher. Third, in most competitions, the gymnast only gets one vault. The men thus are forced to take the one and only execution as the counting score. If the male gymnast makes a mistake, he is stuck with the score.

The vaulting for men begins with a run of 20 meters, about 10 feet shorter than the women's run. The men also have a toe board beyond which they cannot run.

The vaults included here are the Tsukahara with a full twist in a tuck position and a handspring front somersault with a half twist. Both vaults were included in their rudimentary forms in the women's section on vaulting. The reader should be aware that there are many women performing the vaults listed here for the men. These vaults were included because they are often performed by the men at higher level competitions and are most likely to see continued progress and adaptation.

Tuck Tsukahara with a Full Twist

The tuck Tsukahara with a full twist shown here is being performed from the near end of the horse as opposed to the far end (Fig. 42). The gymnast shows how very low to the horse the preflight is and how bent the first arm is at horse contact. The round-off portion of the vault is shown in the second and third photos as the gymnast pushes from the horse into a high tuck position above the horse.

The gymnast is twisting in the same direction throughout the entire vault, twisting left during the preflight and continuing to twist left during the full twist. Other gymnasts do the one-quarter turn onto the horse in one direction followed by a full twisting somersault in the other. This latter method might be called a "tinsica front to barani out" rather than a Tsukahara with a full twist. There are arguments for both techniques and gymnasts learn the vault equally competently by either method. It is important to recognize and understand the difference so that the proper mechanics for each style can be discerned and approached systematically.

It is also important to recognize the few important characteristics of the vault that include: a low and fast preflight; violent push from the second arm onto the horse; and promotion of the somersault phase of the skill. The somersault is what everyone has problems with. The gymnast who can produce enough force to perform the somersault will generally find that the twist really takes very little additional force.

Handspring Front with a Half-Twist

The handspring front somersault with a half-twist is self-explanatory (Fig. 43). The gymnast will use much the same techniques discussed in the women's section on vaulting. The twist portion of the vault is a little more complicated and deserves some discussion. The competitor will begin the twist when he is turning upside down after he has left the horse and begun his tuck. The half-twist at this point allows the gymnast to see the mat and landing spot. This "barani" action, or movement, is familiar to trampolinists but can be particularly difficult to the uninitiated.

The twisting mechanism can be from a variety of families. The most common and the type displayed by the gymnast pictured is that of skillfully using upper and lower segments of the body to provide alternate moments of inertia for the body to twist "against."

Parallel Bars

The parallel bars have been evolving steadily, but undramatically, for many years. The newer skills exhibited on the parallel bars are giant swings between the bars and single-bar work that often resemble high bar or uneven bar skills.

42A

42B

42E

Fig. 42   *Bart Conner shows how
low to the horse in preflight and
how bent the first arm is at horse
contact for a tuck Tsukahara with
a full twist.*

136

42C

42D

42F

137

43A   43B   43C

Fig. 43   *The gymnast begins the twist portion of the handspring front when he is starting to turn upside-down.*

43D   43E

The Diamidov

The Diamidov is a full twisting forward swing to a handstand performed on one arm (Fig. 44). The skill was named after Sergei Diamidov, the first Soviet gymnast to perform it many years ago.

The Diamidov is still a very highly-respected move on parallel bars and marks considerable accomplishment on the part of the gymnast. He begins from a handstand and swings downward and forward very aggressively. About horizontal in the upswing, the gymnast releases one hand and continues the upswing by pushing on the remaining support arm. As the swing continues upward, the gymnast will begin to turn toward the support arm. Once this tilt or twist is established, the gymnast continues in the same fashion until a half-turn is completed and he can reach back around his torso to see the bars and finish the twist. As the twist is completed, he puts his free hand back on the same rail from which he withdrew it and returns to the handstand.

The Diamidov begins from a stutz, which is a swing half-turn instead of a full turn. The stutz involves some flight but does not require the gymnast to swing quite as high as in the Diamidov. The gymnast should begin with the stutz and, as swing and confidence improves, he can continue the upswing higher and higher until the support arm pushes the gymnast near vertical. This type of swing generally takes many years to perfect, but the young gymnast should begin working on it nearly from the first day of approaching the parallel bars.

Underbar Cast

The underbar cast is one of the skills that the gymnast can perform below the bars (Fig. 45). Actually, the gymnast is required to show skills performed both above and below the bars. The cast in the bar exercise is used to propel the gymnast above the bars, below the bars, and eventually to the upper-arm support, or back to a straight-arm support. The gymnast uses the cast in this skill to get support to the upper arms, to be followed by an uprise backward swing and a straddle cut.

The cast in the pictures here is also being done with a rather sophisticated downswing. The gymnast drops below the bars using an early drop method. (Interestingly, the women would probably call this a late drop, because of its general position in most of their routines.) The early drop gives the gymnast substantially more swing than the late drop, in which the gymnast swings entirely forward before leaning backward and then swinging below the bars. The gymnast drops or swings below the bars where he pikes tightly and continues the swing upward and forward in this tight pike position.

Fig. 44 *The Diamidov is a full-twisting forward swing to a handstand on one arm.*

44A

44B

44C

44D

44E

As the swing progresses upward, he releases the bars with both hands and arrives in an upper-arm support that sometimes looks painful but isn't. From this upper-arm position, the gymnast usually swings backward on his upper arms to perform another skill on the backward end of the swing, the uprise to a straddle cut.

The underbar cast shown here is considered elementary in difficulty, but it is used frequently and almost every young gymnast will learn it at some time in his training. The gymnast here shows exemplary technique and the reader is well advised to note how high he has his body position as he catches the bars on his upper arms.

Double Tuck Dismount

The dismount that seems to be the compulsory-optional dismount of modern parallel bars in the double tuck somersault (Fig. 46). This move begins in a handstand from which the gymnast swings downward and forward very aggressively.

The gymnast swings upward and forward even more recklessly than the Diamidov to release roughly at horizontal and then adopts the tuck position that he will hold for the remaining 1¾ somersaults to land on the mat at the side of the bars.

A small amount of force must be directed to move the body sideward to avoid coming down on the bars. This is not really difficult, except for the combination of swings required for the gymnast to rise high enough without collapsing. He must swing quickly enough to somersault fast, and still have a little force available to move sideward to avoid landing on the rail.

Horizontal Bar

Where does one begin on the horizontal bar? It has become such an intricate and spectacular event that just to show all the spectacular releases would take hundreds of pages.

The horizontal bar exercise must include swings that move around the bar and special types of swings together with releases and regrasps. Some of the more elementary swings have already been included in the section on women's uneven bars and will not be repeated here. The horizontal bar affords such large swings that the potential for developing huge amounts of force and using this force for doing other skills is well within the reach of most gymnasts.

Fig. 45 *The underbar cast is considered elementary, but it is frequently used and a requirement for almost every competitor.*

45A

45D

45E

45B

45C

45F

45G

46A

46B

46E

Fig. 46 *The gymnast must apply a certain amount of force to move sideward to avoid a collision with the bars when ending the double tuck dismount.*

46C

46D

46F

46G

47A   47B

Fig. 47   *The artistic Hecht dismount shown here is presently a compulsory skill in gymnastics. A prerequisite is a release that will lift the gymnast high into the air.*

Hecht Dismount

The first skill to be covered here is the Hecht dismount, which shows some of the intricacies of swing in the horizontal bar (Fig. 47).

The skillful gymnast can change the natural circular motion of the giant swing by piking and arching. The upswing shown in the photos demonstrates a slight pike as the gymnast passes the bottom of the swing, followed by an arch and a release that lifts him high above the bar. These types of body position changes and skill actions are extremely important for the horizontal bar and afford the gymnast the opportunity to utilize his swing in such fashions as to make his releases higher, freer, and with more ease.

The Hecht here is the present compulsory dismount but has been used for years and may be considered basic.

146

47C

47F   47G

47D

47E

48A   48B

Fig. 48 *Mario McCutcheon demonstrates a one-arm reverse Hecht, a spectacular evolution from the regular Hecht.*

One-Arm Reverse Hecht

This skill is such a remarkable achievement that we could not resist including it (Fig. 48).

The swings on horizontal bar have progressed to the point that gymnasts are actually doing giant swings, turns, dismounts, and releases and regrasps using only one arm. This has been facilitated by using those unusual grips with the dowels and much work on sophisticated swing techniques, but, all in all, the sky's the limit on the high bar.

A reverse hecht has some fancy arching and piking in it. Until recently, a reverse hecht from two hands was considered very difficult; to perform the skill from one arm is amazing. The reader should note the pike in the downswing, arch in the upswing, and the timing of the release.

Full-In - Full-Out Dismount

You know what a half-in - half-out dismount is from the still rings. So looking at it in the same light, you might think that a full-in - full-out contains a

48C   48D   48E

48F   48G

Fig. 49 *The full-in full-out dismount on the horizontal bar is closely related to the same skill in the rings. The gymnast here is twisting in a puck position, which is a cross between a tuck and a pike.*

full-in in the first somersault and a full-out in the second somersault. That's pretty close (Fig. 49).

Interestingly, the gymnast uses the two somersaults to combine the twists in a variety of different fractions of turns. The dismount is pictured beginning at the release. The gymnast performs one full twist in the first somersault, another in the second, flies high during the whole process, and lands well under control about fifteen feet from the bar. The giant swing before this type of dismount is accelerated to very high speed as the gymnast pikes more tightly during the upswing to bring his body over the bar with greater velocity. By accelerating the giant swings, he can build up more speed to be used in making the dismount go higher and farther. This allows him to perform the dismounts of this nature where there is more than one turn or more than two somersaults.

The gymnast here is twisting in a "puck" position. While not a very attractive name, it indicates a cross between a tuck and a pike. This body position allows the gymnast to twist and somersault with nearly equal degrees of ease. Although the puck position is not particularly elegant in still photography, during the actual full speed execution of the skill you will not see it as easily. The puck gets lost in the high-speed blur of so much happening at one time. Yet, the elegance of its engineering is something to behold.

49C

49D

49E

49F

6

TRAINING: A DOZEN IMPORTANT QUESTIONS ANSWERED

Learning is supposed to go from the simple to the complex, from the easy to the difficult. Gymnastics is one of the most obvious sports in which to apply this principle.

Gymnastics skills are relatively easy to understand, gymnasts are generally quite skilled, and the movements are generally observable from film or watching more competent gymnasts perform. As you've seen, the skills of gymnastics have been given names and even the sub-skills or parts of skills often have names. This makes the teaching and learning of gymnastics quite straightforward.

There is an old saying that goes: If at first you don't succeed, divide the problem. If you still don't succeed, divide again. This division of effort, or compartmentalization, if you will, is the cornerstone of effective learning and teaching in gymnastics. The teacher and student of gymnastics should be aware of the parts of skills and the relative contribution of each. This vital consideration helps keep the gymnast safe and allows him or her to move easily from the simple to the complex.

The gymnast's education must proceed by first learning the alphabet of gymnastics, which includes skills such as handstands, bridges, splits, rolling, turning, somersaulting, and twisting. These individual efforts are then put together in more and more complex ways. The ability of the gymnast to perform these basic skills is very important and progress should be delayed until full competence is demonstrated in each. This is a difficult concept for modern athletes, many of whom desire progress so impatiently. Since our society demands instant coffee, instant hamburgers, instant communication, and instant results, our athletics also suffers from this demand. The long and painstaking development of skills in gymnastics demands a teacher who is 100%

dedicated to fully competent realization of each and every phase of a skill. The young gymnast seeking a competent coach should look carefully for this quality. The overzealous coach who can claim "instant" success is simply not honest. The young gymnast will be wise to select a coach who has been training athletes for many years at the level to which the athlete aspires. The gymnast and coach should constantly and consistently check and recheck every step.

Learning of physical skills is developed in habit patterns. As the gymnast performs repetition after repetition, he or she is training the body to perform exactly what is repeated. If the gymnast repeats errors, a bad habit becomes nearly unbreakable, and the gymnast will become extremely limited. The safety of gymnasts depends most intimately on the teacher and student being careful to take each step and savor the learning carefully so that no holes are left in development. Any shortcuts or neglected skills will only come back to haunt the athlete.

Here are some of the most common questions asked by aspiring gymnasts and their parents:

1. How do you know when to start the young child in gymnastics?

Answer: When the child shows an interest in beginning gymnastics classes. This can be encouraged by finding a competent and child-centered teacher and program in your local area. The youngest age of participation in the gymnastics seen on television is around 8 or 9 (Fig. 50). Prior to this time, young athletes can participate in classes and take dance without subjecting themselves to all of the rigors of high intensity and high impact gymnastics.

2. How do you select the appropriate program for a child?

Answer: We never want to close doors for young people by limiting what they can accomplish. This means that we should always place children in programs that are very mobile, that is, programs that can take the child where he or she wants to go if the child shows the inclination, dedication, ability, and determination to achieve at higher levels. The entire family should be comfortable with the goals and conduct of the program. Failure to achieve this kind of harmony often causes friction.

One way to judge a program is to see how many high-level athletes it has produced. But you can evaluate the program on many more dimensions than simple productivity. For example:

    A. The coach should have worked with athletes in the past who have competed at the level of aspiration of the child.

    B. The program should have a section devoted to the lateral arabesques in the "Peter Principle," or, in other words, provide a spot for children who do not pan out as top-notch competitors. This means that, if the children do not make it, they have a place in the program where they can enjoy gymnastics at their own level of competence and remain challenged and productive.

C. The child should have some opportunity to work with the best coaches in the program. The child in the beginning levels should be working at times with the top-level or most talented coach. We often see productive programs that are effective at high levels because of the ability and energy of one particular coach. One of the considerations of finding a program for each child is that the participant will be able to work with the most skillful coaches part of the time.

D. The program should have access to the following types of additional personnel: orthopedist, podiatrist, psychologist, dietician, trainer, biomechanist, and exercise physiologist (these last two monitor athletes to prevent overtraining). These people will be the resources the coach and athlete will use to solve problems that are beyond their own capabilities. The coach cannot be the answer to everything for everyone. Interestingly, the best athletes usually come up with the most exotic problems and need some very high-powered experts for them. These auxiliary personnel will often spell the difference between success and failure and every quality program should have them available for the athletes within 24 hours.

E. The program should have enough equipment that the gymnast does not have to stand in line for very long. The gymnast's ability to learn and his or her later consistency of performance are usually determined by the number and quality of repetitions that the athlete was able to complete during training.

F. The time involved in training or education is largely determined by the determination, sustained interest, and desires of the athlete. The length of classes or training should be short enough so the gymnast is reluctant to leave, thus ensuring the desire to return the next day. The practice and classes should always be run very efficiently so that not one minute is wasted and the athletes can get all of their work done in the shortest amount of time. This allows the athletes an ample amount of time to do the other things that make them happy and good students.

G. The program should keep extensive and accurate records on the progress and abilities of the athletes. Record keeping, in every endeavor, is the most often overlooked. By not keeping accurate records of training, conditioning, and other activities, we are all destined to forget what worked and repeat mistakes.

3. **Do gymnasts need to take dance classes?**

Answer: You better believe it, both men and women. The dance training involved in ballet and related areas can help the gymnast develop elegance and presence. The areas of dance that help the female gymnast are self-evi-

Fig. 50 *These young girls are off to an early, good start. The typical age for many beginners is 8 years old.*

dent. The female must use her dance training to fulfill requirements necessary to compete. In essence, the gymnast who dances the best, along with the other requirements in floor exercise and beam, should win. Therefore, developing good dance will help you win.

The male gymnast is not usually very anxious to participate in dance training. However, one look at some of the training of foreign gymnasts will tell you that they have had some form of dance instruction. Dance is the singular most basic form of human movement for its own sake, movement that is justified by its very beauty and skill. Gymnastics is an exercise in beauty of movement with an emphasis on daring and athleticism.

4. Is it true that gymnasts have been taking drugs to stunt their growth?

Answer: No. The use of drugs is not very helpful to the gymnast. Although some drugs will enhance the performance of the "all-out" types of sports, they usually have side effects that can only harm the gymnast. The gymnast does not need all-out endurance, but endurance under control. He or she does not need all-out power but power under control. The gymnast must be in such exquisite control of his or her faculties that anything that disturbs this control will spell disaster.

The fact that gymnasts often develop physically a little later than other athletes is only due to the fact that they work harder to keep their weight down.

The male gymnasts tend to be late in maturing and small when compared to athletes in many other sports. The female gymnasts also tend to be small and lean. The delayed menstruation attributed to the female gymnast has been shown to occur in other sports that have a high energy output and thus a low fat-to-weight ratio, which appears to delay the onset of menses. The national average age for the first menses of the female is around 12.5 years. There are many female gymnasts who do not menstruate until well into their late teens. This appears to be simply a delay, not a medical problem.

5. How much does it cost to train in gymnastics?

Answer: It varies, of course, but costs can range from $2.00 per hour to around $6.00 per hour for class-level instruction—or about $75.00 to $500.00 per month for higher level training. The university and school level gymnasts can train for free.

6. Should gymnasts consider weight training to enhance their performance or should they rely on the constant repetition of skills to acquire strength?

Answer: There are proponents of both ideas. In our opinion, the day has gone when the gymnasts can train to their maximum ability only by doing their skills. Gymnastics as a sport is one of the few that still clings to traditional ideas of training that may or may not hold up to sound scrutiny. Gymnastics is still one of the few sports that is not literally won in the weight room.

There are some restrictions for weight training, especially when the child is particularly young. Some evidence indicates that the very young athlete should not train with very heavy weights or high resistances because of the stress and strain on developing growth centers and because of relatively fragile ligament and tendon construction. Much still has to be learned in this area, but there are many good texts available on weight training and you should try to find these to seek out the most recent and trusted information.

7. Is there a special diet that gymnasts must eat to keep slim and maintain their strength?

Answer: This is always an interesting question. Many people still do not understand the contribution of nutrition to athletic training. The old idea of the basic food groups and eating a balanced diet that everyone learned in health class years ago in elementary school has not changed significantly. In fact, it is obvious that the most important information that we can give our athletes about nutrition is that if you eat a balanced diet and do not neglect any of the food groups you will have all of what you need to train effectively.

It is also obvious that few athletes and coaches believe this as they all try everything from Vitamin E to bee pollen in a quest for the perfect diet. Vitamins are simply catalysts for chemical reactions already taking place in the body. The body can synthesize only a rather small amount of protein and extra-large protein intakes will not help to increase strength. The simple fact that athletes must keep their weight under control indicates that they simply cannot overeat, something hard to do in modern America.

8. In order to receive the finest training, do you have to send the young gymnast miles away from home?

Answer: Moving away from home should only be done as a last resort. Granted, there are a few coaches in the country who are considered "Champion Builders." However, this concept is a little overused and needs to be examined. The desire and determination to be a champion must come from the child, not the coach. The coach does not make the champions; he or she merely guides the process. An old track and field coach once said: "Last year I was the best track coach in the country, and then he graduated."

In our opinion, most children should stay home whenever possible to train. Unfortunately, there are not enough really high-level, determined coaches, and there is usually not enough money to provide programs necessary to foster this high level. Sometimes the child may have to move to another training circumstance to enjoy the benefits of a more ambitious and panoramic program.

Before moving, the parent and child should consider the cost since a step upward in a program is often a step upward in expense. The cost of travel and getting to and from the gym may be very prohibitive. The family might, indeed, weigh the cost of what it would take to move to this new program and then consider what might happen if they took this extra money and fed it into the existing program. This extra money might just put the local program on a par with the one they want to move to.

9. How do you get a skill named after you, such as the Thomas Flair, Korbut Back, or Tsukahara vault?

Answer: The skill must be done by the gymnast for the first time in either World or Olympic competition. It is a great honor to have a skill named after you and it can be quite intimidating for other athletes. It is pretty unnerving when you're standing in line getting ready to warm up your Voronin on the high bar when Voronin is in front of you in line!

10. What is spotting?

Answer: During competitions and training, you can often see a coach assisting gymnasts through a skill by touching them as they take off or catching them when they are near the floor. This manipulation of the gymnast's body by another person is called spotting.

The spotter's purpose is to prevent unnecessary hard landings, assist the gymnast through a skill so that he or she can "feel" the actions, or prevent accidental falls. The job is difficult and dangerous. The spotter must have a fair amount of reckless abandon as he or she jumps in to catch the falling gymnast, and considerable skill in manipulating a heavy body through the air to complete a skill safely. The spotter is often struck by the arms and legs of the gymnast. The gymnast often owes his or her safety and well-being to the quick-thinking spotter who rushed in to rescue a poor attempt. Spotting seems to move in and out of fashion; some coaches and gymnasts, at times, spot everything, while there are some who take such painstaking progressions that they do not spot at all. Both systems have proven successful. However, much less spotting is done now than in years past.

11. Where do you go to learn to be a gymnastics coach?

Answer: In most cases, your gymnastics coach was a former gymnast and he or she might have some knowledge about the sport that comes from having participated as a competitor. As for more formal education in the coaching art, the typical route is for a young coach to work as an assistant under a knowledgeable and experienced master coach until such time as the young assistant is ready and able to venture out to set up his or her own program. This sort of apprenticeship program for coaches is useful, but does not always do the best job, particularly if the master is a specialist without a wide variety of experiences.

In our present gymnastics environment, most coaches come to coaching directly out of college and directly from competing. The young coach enters an environment where the young gymnast may not be talented, may not ultimately survive the attrition process, and may not be competing for years. We should have an extended period of "internship" for all coaches with a master coach. In this internship, the coaches would no longer be training, as in the apprenticeship program, but actually coaching.

Although the young coach is entering a very challenging and competitive environment, the stimulation of the challenge cannot outweigh the responsibility of dealing with the children or young adults who are looking to the coach for knowledge.

12. What about anorexia and bulimia in female gymnasts?

Answer: These dietary and metabolic disorders seem to show up in women's gymnastics quite frequently, but investigators have found that they are also widely spread through other sports and activities. It is doubtful that gymnastics is the cause of any such disorders. The individuals who develop such disorders bring their particular personalities and problems to gymnastics rather than getting them from the sport. The dietary restrictions for keeping the weight under control can be taken to fanatical ends, like most anything.

WHAT IS INTERNATIONAL COMPETITION LIKE?

Most young gymnasts dream of becoming international stars and representing the United States in foreign competition. This dream is realized every year by about twenty men and women artistic gymnasts and a similar number of rhythmic gymnasts.

This is a rather small number of athletes to send out of the country and the reason is that there are only a few ready for such competition. Also, there are only a small number of events in which the United States participates. The Europeans compete country-to-country more than the United States does, largely due to their geographical advantages.

To be a part of this select group, the young gymnast must first become a member of the national team. This number varies from year to year, although approximately 20 usually get assigned an international contest.

The United States team is picked at the National Championships for Elite level gymnasts. The number of athletes participating in these championships is usually between twenty and fifty, depending upon whether there are junior-level Elites (fourteen years and under) involved or not.

In the Championships of the USA, the athletes are ranked from No. 1 through the last place to determine international meet assignment or qualification to any trials to select a special team for the Olympics, World Championships, Pan American Games, or World University Games.

The Championships of the USA may be the last ranking for that period of the year if there are no trials. If there are trials, the top athletes will compete and be ranked again to select the top seven or eight to travel to the international event.

Men have traditionally been selected almost strictly by rank alone. Women are chosen according to rank and the strategy of the national coach and his assistants. The rank attained by the gymnast usually determines the meets that the athlete will be invited to attend. For example, the most prestigious competitions abroad are offered to the highest ranks first. The less prestigious or remaining important competitions are then offered to whomever is still eligible, whomever may need the international experience, or both.

The U. S. gymnast with a rank in the top ten can usually count on being offered a trip to another country as a member of the national squad for dual competition or as an individual to an international invitational. Once the offer is made, the athlete and coach can choose to accept or reject it according to training, rest and school requirements, prestige of the competition, and other factors. There are a number of times when athletes do, in fact, turn down competitions abroad. Most athletes and coaches look upon international competition as a privilege.

Why would anyone turn down an opportunity to travel abroad? Let's look at what actually happens to the international gymnast in preparing and attending these competitions. It is not all fun and games, but it still can be a very rewarding experience.

The athlete who accepts a trip abroad must first get a uniform. He or she must also get a passport and sometimes a visa as well, which means procuring pictures, forms, and birth records.

The competitions are not usually communicated to the U. S. Gymnastics Federation until only a few weeks prior to the actual meet. That means the athletes and the Federation really have to hustle to get ready and get all the paper work done. Then, the gymnast might suffer a last-minute injury. This may put the USGF in a bind if the coach doesn't notify the committee early enough so that an alternate can be named. The replacement, in turn, may be delighted to get a trip overseas, but may not have had adequate preparation time.

The gymnast scheduled for international competition often must notify his or her school that he/she is going to be gone. Most trips take over a week, and the gymnast must then make up all the school work missed.

It is not often that the gymnast will travel with his or her personal coach. Usually, athletes and coaches are assigned at the same time and may never have worked together before. The success of the competition can often be decided by how well and how quickly the gymnast and the coach get to know each other. The coach may have to deal with an athlete trained by habits completely different from those he or she uses. Discipline, personal idiosyncracies, training habits, emotions, and other problems that the athlete's personal coach has well in hand may become new problems for the young athlete going abroad with a new coach for the first time.

The gymnast usually meets other athletes in New York or Los Angeles prior to going abroad. Once the athletes are on the plane and ready to go, they must be responsible for their passport, visa, training gear, music, and other supplies. Every athlete who goes abroad more than five or six times most likely will have his or her luggage lost at one time or another. One U.S. group in Bulgaria never did get their luggage back. They had to borrow clothes and wash them daily!

Sometimes the long flights are absolutely exhausting. On a recent trip to China, the gymnasts were on the plane for over thirty hours. Due to bad weather in London, gymnasts on their way to the Coca-Cola Invitational were on the same plane for thirty-six hours. Of course, missing planes is also a problem. Two U.S. gymnasts had to spend a night in Amsterdam alone because the coach had caught a different flight home to a much different part of the country and the kids missed their flight.

The jet lag can really confuse gymnasts. They may not be tired when it's time to sleep and they do need to rest to perform their best. Their eating schedules are all out of sync. They may also risk upper respiratory infections. Then, gymnasts may find foreign food strange, distasteful, or even nauseating. They almost always discover that there are not many all-night grocery stores abroad, television is boring because you cannot understand what they are saying, and, if you're in a Communist country, there may not be a television set for a hundred miles. There may be no video games for weeks and you might run out of clean clothes.

If you become sick abroad, getting medical care may sometimes be a real problem. In the Soviet Union, when U.S. gymnast John Crosby had an attack of appendicitis, he was taken by Soviet authorities to the hospital and became "property" of the physician until he was released. The U.S. delegation had some trouble locating him. In a recent trip to East Germany, one athlete became ill and was taken to the hospital for tests overnight. If you think going to the hospital is scary, imagine going when no one speaks English and cannot tell you what is happening!

Then, as if all this were not enough, there may be more of a home court advantage than we might like. The equipment may not be as good as in the United States, or at least it may be very different. The floor mat may be hard, the boards dead, and the rails slow.

With all these problems, why do we go? Because it's fun (Fig. 51).

All the problems listed above are small nuisances compared to the tremendous learning experiences for young athletes who go abroad. We have never seen an athlete yet who returned from a Communist country who was not changed by the experience. Athletes do not get much chance to do the kind of sightseeing a normal tourist does, but they usually do get to know a few new people. Watching the way other countries perform the same functions that we do can make a young gymnast much more cosmopolitan. They also acquire a larger degree of tolerance for the habits of others. The fact that the athlete is actually the foreigner makes the young gymnast more aware of his or her personality and willingness to be an ambassador of good will. The actual competition may be a small part of the total picture.

The sightseeing on international trips is usually limited by tourist standards but most gymnasts take the opportunity to see local places of interest. Sometimes they may even be able to take a short sojourn in another part of the country if the return is delayed a day or two. The athletes are usually treated with some dignity while abroad and occasionally are allowed special privileges in seeing things that even the natives cannot see.

Of course, the opportunity to see the Kremlin, Great Wall of China, pyramids, Mount Fuji, and the Hawaiian Islands is far better than reading about them in a book and these are some of the sights that will live with the gymnast forever.

Fig. 51   *A budding U.S. star learns what it's like to be the center of attention.*

It is very common to exchange gifts with opposing athletes, coaches, and meet administrators. The generosity of each country is almost a competition itself as many look upon their generosity in gift giving as a means of topping the other countries and making the trip a truly enjoyable experience. The athletes have returned with glass from West Germany, fine linens from Amsterdam, carvings from China, and clothes from South America.

Best of all, since the trip is free for the athlete, the price is right. The athlete's food, room, and transportation are funded by the governing body or by the host federation. The gymnasts are roomed by country and a devoted number of fans generally follow them nearly everywhere they go.

Returning home is sometimes hard. Athletes grow to be fast friends and may even send each other gifts through other countrymen. This friendship has resulted in gymnasts becoming long standing pen-pals, visiting outside of gymnastics, and enjoying growth experiences unlikely ever to be paralleled in academic institutions.

Often the athlete returns home to a pile of homework, but the storehouse of memories makes the trip worthwhile. The support that these athletes require, and seldom get, as they go abroad, makes the role of the schools and the national system more and more important. Traveling internationally for most people is quite out of their financial reach and traveling as an athlete gives the talented gymnast an opportunity to see other parts of the world and to grow from the experience.

By supporting the athletes who compete abroad we not only get better athletes but better citizens. They come home a little older, a little tired, and a lot wiser.

8

AN INTERVIEW WITH MAS WATANABE,

U.S. National Program Director for Men, Conducted by Bill Sands

Bill: How is the Men's Program structured?

Mas: The typical structure right now is that the gymnast begins at a local club and then moves into a more structured and higher-level local club. Then the gymnast moves into the Junior Olympic program. That is the normal process, but it used to be a little bit different. It used to be that the public school system was a little stronger. There were even junior high school programs as well as high school programs. The public school system had a broader base and was able to get to the most athletes. The current trend is more toward getting the athletes into a private club.

The public high schools have been dropping gymnastics programs, but the clubs have begun picking up these athletes, although not the large numbers that used to be participating in the high school. The sheer number of athletes in men's gymnastics has declined but the Junior Olympic program for the U.S. Gymnastics Federation has had a significant increase in the number of young men participating.

Bill: How many gymnasts does the USGF have competing in the men's program?

Mas: I believe around 6,000 are registered and have competed. However, this does not represent the actual number since the largest number of athletes is at the Class IV or lowest level. There is a new Class V level low enough that most young boys can begin competing rather early, but the Class V gymnasts do not yet register with the USGF. This number also does not include high school athletes, nor all of the other programs available to young boys. The number could possibly be doubled or tripled to indicate the actual total of male gymnasts training in the United States.

The gymnasts start on the club level, enter the Junior Olympic program, and stay there until they are just below the senior level, which is our Olympic level. So, as far as the gymnast is concerned, he can stay in the Junior Olympic program until he enters college. Then 90% of the boys become collegiate gymnasts and enter the senior program, which is really a university program and coexists with the NCAA.

The senior program is composed of 70 percent collegiate and NCAA athletes, about 25 percent of whom are post-graduate gymnasts or gymnasts who have ended their college eligibility and are finishing up their degree program. Then, about 5 percent stay out of college to continue to train with their clubs through the first part of their college years.

Bill: Can you summarize then, the typical route a boy might follow from the beginning of his gymnastics training until entering international competition?

Mas: The typical route might be to join a local gymnastics club and thus become introduced to gymnastics before entering a competitive program. The young boy can actually enter a competitive program very quickly if he is a little talented or has a few skills. Then, he can be introduced to competition at the Class V level.

Then, the boys move up to classes in a very structured way by their age and their ability level. For instance, Class I has only one age division, 16–18. If you are 13 you cannot be in Class I. Class II consists of both the 13–15 and 16–18 age groups. However, at the nationals, only age 16–18 Class I's and 13–15 Class II's compete.

Bill: Is the men's program much more strict about structure and age grouping than the women's program?

Mas: Yes, because of the gymnast's physical maturity. The young boys mature much more slowly than the girls and the program and skills demanded of the different ages and ability levels match their physical ability and development very well.

Bill: What is your background?

Mas: My competitive background was as a member of the national team of Japan. They pick the top twelve every year. I made the team from 1963 to '68. In 1963 I was a member of the World University Games team, placing third. In 1969, I was selected to go someplace else and I did not attend the World University Games but did qualify for the team. The best year I had was in 1966, in which I was the World Championships team alternate. I was 5th all-around and placed first on the high bar, second on rings, and third on the parallel bars in the all-Japan Championships. I retired in 1968 after the Olympic Trials.

I started my coaching career in 1969 after my competitive retirement in Berkeley, California. I was assistant coach at Berkeley from 1969 to 1977. During that period, our team was NCAA champion once, second once, and third once. George Greenfield made the Olympic team and Tom Weeden and Tom

Beach made the World Championships team.

In 1974, I also started to direct a local club. The club lasted for three years. During those three years I coached Tracee Talavera and Julianne McNamara. I worked with girls because there were many more of them. I was just finishing up my master's program from 1972 to 1974 when I got a little side-tracked as I started my club and had to see that the club ran properly and that everything would work well. The club had to start in September and my thesis had to be done at the same time. I am presently a thesis away from a master's degree.

In 1974, when I had the job offer for starting the gym club, I had realized that my original assumption about where I should be in the gymnastics community was not appropriate. When I came from Japan, I thought that I should be at the college level because that was where I would have the most effect. After a few years of working with the college-age and senior-level athletes, I found that this was not true. I needed to get to the gymnasts before they got to the college level. By the time I had gymnasts in the collegiate program, I found that they were very hard to change, their basics were so bad, and I could not make enough changes in their work to do the kind of gymnastics that I wanted.

In 1974 I started the Junior Olympic program for boys. It was that year that we had our first Junior Olympic National Championships and began the compulsory exercises. I composed the compulsory exercises for the USGF age group program. There was a compulsory program at this time, but it was not used very widely and was not very popular. At this time we made the Class I and Class II compulsory watered-down versions of the Olympic compulsory. Then Class III and Class IV were composed of basic skills. This concept was effective and was received well. At the beginning, it was difficult because the skill level was not very high and I had to make the exercises rather simple compared to what we have now. As far as the overall concept, the Class I compulsory should be related to the Olympic compulsory and the Class II should be a lead-up to the Class I compulsory. This concept has helped us greatly over the past eight or nine years.

Bill: Can you tell me what you do for the USGF now in your present position as national program director for men?

Mas: I was hired in 1977 as program director for men. At the time we did not have a women's program director. When I was hired the job was very new and I had to create my own job description. So I did work for the women's side a little bit with training camps and some other things.

Eventually, I became just the program director for men. Most of my job, 90% or so, is dealing with the Junior Olympic program. Most of the administration and restructuring of this program was, and still is a large part of my job. Of course, the NCAA took care of most of the administration of the Senior Program so I didn't really have to touch too much of this program. The needs of the Junior Olympic program were considerably greater than the needs of the senior program. If events came up, I helped run them and also ran training camps, and conducted clinics and symposia for all aspects of the USGF programs.

I concentrate on the Junior Program. I believe very strongly that the young coaches must work the young boys correctly from the very beginning. I wanted to get in touch with the younger coaches who were more eager and perhaps had more access to the younger boys. This was the key to the whole thing. Because of this emphasis, I think we are now just starting to see the results of this concept. When we began we fully understood that it would take a long time, many years, to get to the place where we are now.

Bill: I think your junior program has gone about structuring itself and its development in the right way. Unlike the women's program, you have looked upon the junior progran as an investment and not a purchase. Is there anything else besides the Junior Program you would like to discuss?

Mas: We are trying to provide more opportunities for seniors in this program. You see, in the past most of the gymnasts who participated during the post-graduate period had problems because skills declined, their rate of improvement slowed, it was harder to stay interested, college coaches did not want to spend much time with them because they were no longer contributing to the NCAA efforts, and they did not have many goals.

Without the collegiate pressures of the NCAA, the men lost sight of their goals and were not stimulated into competing and learning at higher and higher levels. They were not work-oriented unless they were very established gymnasts. There were some exceptional cases like Bart Conner and Kurt Thomas, but some of the others lost their goals and their motivation. They also needed to have enough money to live on and enough time available to train. But most importantly, it was difficult for them to get to good coaching. This forced them to create their own program.

These hardships started their decline, and have been key to our lack of progress during this age period. It is a shame for us that we cannot keep postgraduates competing for these last few years when they will peak physically and developmentally. These are the years in which we lose most of our gymnasts.

When we have a post-graduate program complete, plus the collegiate program and Junior Olympic program, then we will be complete and have a total approach. Then we will be able to watch the gymnasts and control their development from the very beginning all the way through their post-graduate and peaking years. Then you will really be able to tell the total effectiveness of the program.

Bill: What do you think that gymnastics has to offer young men that most

other sports do not have to offer? In particular, what about the "sissy" reputation that has bothered the sport in the past?

Mas: I think that there is a definite wrong notion about gymnastics, that it
is a strictly female type of movement. Determination, courage, daring to do
the skills, and other qualities that we prize in athletes like boxers, must be
present in gymnastics, and with recognition of this fact, finally, I think we
have overcome that sissy image. I do not have the background for why this
image came about, but I think that gymnastics offers men the opportunity to
be artistic as well as masculine.

I used to think that gymnastics was just for the small individual. But I am
beginning to realize that this is incorrect. I looked at the Cubans and saw how
big they are, how strong they are, and that they are very capable of handling
their weight and size. You look at an American sport like football and basketball, and see how quick and strong these athletes are. I think that we can make
a good gymnast out of a football player. I am not kidding. I have a very strong
feeling about that now. I think we are losing athletes because if the sport
appeals only to small people, then we are cutting off the opportunity for larger
athletes to participate.

I think that being small may be a slight advantage, but if the larger athlete
is strong and quick then he can compete against the smaller athlete just as
well. We might have to change our apparatus specifications but we cannot
limit our athletes by physical size. We can make gymnasts out of bigger
athletes.

Bill: How are the national and Olympic teams selected?

Mas: According to a qualification system that lasts throughout the year.
There are certain meets designated as qualifying meets to higher level meets.
A score is designated as the qualifying score. Then, as the athlete qualifies into
higher meets, he ultimately qualifies for the Championships of the USA where
a certain number of the top ranks are invited to compete in the Olympic Trials
where the actual Olympic team is selected. A certain number of ranks are designated as our national team.

Bill: Can you summarize your concept in developing your junior program?

Mas: I think the most important thing we teach in the junior program is
learning correct basics. This was largely accomplished by the careful selection
of skills for the compulsory exercises. The compulsory exercises measure the
degree of proficiency of each skill. This forces the young boy to work very
hard on each skill and its absolute correct mechanics. This was the main idea
that I used in designing the compulsory exercise and made sure that the
coaches understood why we use them. Now I think we are seeing the results
of this work and are realizing more and more the importance of these
exercises.

Among the junior gymnasts are those who are very talented and need to be directed to a little higher level and maintain the right direction. You must gear some of your emphasis toward the talented athletes and the highest levels.

I offer a national testing program every year. This testing consists of skills that can be the goal of the gymnast who is already very talented and at the highest levels, as well as the less talented gymnasts. The testing program covers skills that are not included in the compulsory exercises but do provide a challenge and incentive to the talented young gymnast who has great potential but may not be quite ready to compete with the older gymnast in his age group or cannot put all his talent to use in performing the more difficult compulsory.

When I started the testing program I could not see the immediate effects but over the years I began to see tremendous influence. The results helped the compulsory program and the optional program. They provided for the extra factors that take a long time to develop but will ultimately serve most or all levels of the young men we need to encourage.

For the talented boys we also have a national team program, our Junior National Team. I use this to help train them and to help provide direction. We provide four weeks of training camps per year. But four weeks is not enough, so we hope to give them direction and extra help in developing their skills and abilities.

We work on correct frame of mind, motivation, and other factors that help develop a complete athlete without over-emphasis on skills. We are truly trying to educate our athletes in all facets of training and gymnastics growth and development. This is why the program has been successful.

Bill: Would you like to make any concluding remarks?

Mas: I really think that the sport of gymnastics has been a vital part of my life. If somebody were to take gymnastics away from me, I would have nothing. I am very proud of myself and my life through gymnastics.

I really learned a great, great deal through gymnastics; I can see how it helped develop my personality and my thought processes. Gymnastics can give you a complete laboratory and environment for the total human being.

We cannot look at the sport as just physical activity. The sport has tremendous potential for learning. We really need to emphasize that this sport can offer so much. It is a total education of the person, not just a recreation.

THE MASTER OF SPORT AWARDS — A GYMNASTICS HALL OF FAME

Unlike many sports associations, the United States Gymnastics Federation does not have a Hall of Fame—something that may be in the offing.

In the meantime, the absence of a Hall of Fame does not mean the Federation fails to recognize the achievements of its many members. The USGF has instead its prestigious Master of Sport award. Thus far there have been seventeen such recipients, all of whom will be shoo-ins if a Hall is ever established.

Here are biographies of the current seventeen USGF Master of Sport honorees:

Bill Crenshaw

A semi-retired operator of two gymnastics clubs and several camps in the Austin, Texas area, Crenshaw was the head coach of the sport at the University of Texas for twenty-three years. He was extremely active in the Amateur Athletic Union before becoming equally instrumental in the development of the USGF while serving on important committees. He is best known for pioneering clubs in the Austin area.

Frank Cumiskey

A three-time Olympian ('32, '36, '48), Cumiskey won over twenty-five national AAU titles before going on to become a top judge at such events as the Pan-American Games, World Championships, and Olympic Games. He was the USGF technical director 1972–77 and has received numerous awards, including induction into the Helms Hall of Fame.

Jackie Fie

An Iowan, Fie was a 1956 Olympian who went on to become a judge at three later Olympic Games and four World Championships. She is one of seven members of the FIG Women's Technical Committee, which is responsible for many regulations governing the sport. She also has written two books about gymnastics and is a frequent lecturer and teacher on the sport.

Joe Giallombardo

Giallombardo won many distinctions as a tumbler in both NCAA and AAU competition in the 1930s and 1940s. He is the recipient of a Helms Hall of Fame certificate from college coaches and was a national and international judge for many years. In 1940, he became the first coach of a suburban high school in Illinois. He currently teaches acrobatics and free exercise in a private studio in Austin, Texas.

Jerry Hardy

A competitor in AAU events from 1926 to 1958, Hardy has been involved in gymnastics for over 50 years and for a while was the national vaulting champion. He coached the U.S. team that competed in the 1956 Pan-American Games and later served as a judge for two World Championships ('58, '66). From 1965 to 1970, he was the U.S. representative to the FIG and since 1957 has written the gymnastics entry in the *Encyclopaedia Britannica.*

George Lewis

Originally a coach of boys' gymnastics, Lewis later specialized in directing girls and, in the process, has developed over thirty national champions. He is known as a pioneer in developing interest among women in the sport on the West Coast and currently coaches at a community college in Seattle, where he also remains active in YMCA programs.

Tom Maloney

Retired and living in Florida, Maloney was the gymnastics coach for the U.S. Military Academy and also has served as the national coordinator for the AAU boys' program. He was the coach of the U.S. teams for the Olympic Games of 1952 and 1960. In 1964, he was the manager for the U.S. team that competed in the Olympics.

Bud Marquette

In his forty-eight-year coaching career, Marquette developed sixteen Olympians, received the Helms Hall of Fame award, and directed the U.S. Olympic Trials of 1968, 1972, and 1976. Most recently, he has been involved with the American Turners National Development program. One of his biggest claims is that he was the founder and director of the first private gymnastics club in the United States—SCATS, first from this country to tour Europe.

George Nissen

One of the latest to receive the USGF's Master of Sport award, this Iowan is famous for his development of the trampoline. The company which bears his name is a leader in producing equipment for the sport. He has been inducted into the Helms Hall of Fame, received the Distinguished Service Award from the President's Council on Physical Fitness, and is honorary president of the International Federation of Trampoline. As a competitor for the University of Iowa, he won national tumbling titles 1935-37.

Charles Pond

The inventor of the Pond Twisting Belt, Pond was the coach of the 1956 Olympic team for the United States and has also developed positions for four men and four women to spots on teams that competed in the Games. At the

University of Illinois, his squads won four NCAA team titles and eleven Big 10 championships.

Mildred Prchal

Prchal's long career has revolved around the American Sokol Organization, for which she was the first female coach. She was the director of the Sokol National Board of Instructors for women for twelve years. Lately, she has become involved with Rhythmic Gymnastics and led the U.S. team to the 1973 Rhythmic World Championships.

Glenn Sundby

Following a colorful career as a show business tumbler and handstand specialist (he was featured in Ripley's "Believe It or Not" for walking down every step of the Washington Monument on his hands), Sundby made an especially big mark in gymnastics as a publisher of magazines. His first, *Acrobat,* folded before his *Modern Gymnast* became the forerunner to the famed *International Gymnast.* His support of the move to create the USGF was considered vital in the federation's pioneer days.

George Szypula

Head coach at Michigan State University, Szypula has developed nearly twenty national individual champions and close to fifty in the Big 10. He also coached the Michigan State team to a national title and has served on many important committees for the sport, including the Helms Foundation Hall of Fame and the Citizens Home Savings Hall of Fame.

Erna Wachtel

A Chicagoan, Wachtel was coach for the U.S. Olympic team in 1956 after a distinguished career as a competitor in which she garnered approximately 100 awards for her skills, including a national Turners All-Around title. She is a former member of the U.S. Olympic Gymnastics Committee and has been extremely active as a teacher of the sport in the Chicago Park District programs.

Lyle Welser

Welser has been a pioneer worker in developing gymnastics in the southeastern United States, where he conducted the first AAU regional competition, served as head coach at Georgia Tech, founded the Georgia Gymnastics Association, and founded the first gymnastics clinic in Daytona, Florida. In addition, he has served on many important committees in the sport.

Gene Wettstone

A 38-year coach at Penn State, Wettstone also served as U.S. coach for the Olympics in 1948 and 1956, and as team manager in 1976. He was also an Olympic judge in 1952 and 1968. At Penn State, he helped develop thirteen Olympians and thirty-seven individual NCAA champions as well as many championship teams. From 1960 to 1972, he headed the U.S. national team. Currently, he helps run numerous international events.

CHAMPIONSHIP HIGHLIGHTS

WOMEN

World Championships

1934, Budapest
TEAM
1, Czechoslovakia; 2, Hungary; 3, Poland.
INDIVIDUAL
All-around: 1, Dekanova, Czechoslovakia; 2, Koloczay, Hungary; 3, Skyrlinska, Poland.

1938, Prague
TEAM
1, Czechoslovakia; 2, Yugoslavia; 3, Poland.
INDIVIDUAL
All-around: 1, Dekanova, Czechoslovakia; 2, Vjerzimirzkova, Czechoslovakia; 3, Palfyeva, Czechoslovakia.

Vault; 1, Palfyeva, Czechoslovakia; 2, Majovska, Poland; 3, Sket, Yugoslavia.

Uneven Bars: 1, Dekanova, Czechoslovakia; 2, Foltova, Czechoslovakia; 3, Dobesova, Czechoslovakia.

Balance Beam: 1, Dekanova, Czechoslovakia; 2, Sket, Yugoslavia; 3, Palfyeva, Czechoslovakia.

Floor Exercise; 1, Palfeyva, Czechoslovakia; 2, Vjerzimirzkova, Czechoslovakia; 3, Foltova, Czechoslovakia.

1950, Basel
TEAM
1, Sweden; 2, France; 3, Italy.
INDIVIDUAL
All-around; 1, Rakoczi, Poland; 2, Peterson, Sweden; 3, Kollar, Austria.

Vault: 1, Rakoczi, Poland; 2, Kollar, Austria; 3, Lemoine, France.

Uneven Bars or Rings: 1, Kollar, Austria; 2, Peterson, Sweden; 3, Rakoczi, Poland.

(Women were changing from rings to uneven bars during this time period and were allowed to perform on either one.)

Balance Beam: 1, Rakoczi, Poland; 2, Nutt, Italy; 3, Machini, Italy.

Floor Exercise: 1, Rakoczi, Poland; 2, Kocia, Yugoslavia; 3, Reindlowa, Poland.

1954, Rome
TEAM
1, Soviet Union; 2, Hungary; 3, Czechoslovakia.
INDIVIDUAL
All-around: 1, Rudjko, USSR; 2, Bosakova, Czechoslovakia; 3, Rakoczi, Poland.

Vault: 1, Manjina, USSR: 2, Peterson, Sweden; 3, Bergen, Sweden.

Uneven Bars: 1, Keleti, Hungary; 2, Rudjko, USSR; 3, Rakoczi, Poland.

Balance Beam: 1, Tanaka, Japan; 2, Bosakova, Czechoslovakia; 3, Keleti, Hungary.

Floor Exercise: 1, Manjina, USSR; 2, Bosakova, Czechoslovakia; 3, Gorokhovskaya, USSR.

1958, Moscow
TEAM
1, USSR; 2, Czechoslovakia; 3, Rumania.
INDIVIDUAL
All-around: 1, Latinjina, USSR; 2, Bosakova, Czechoslovakia; 3, Manjina, USSR.

Vault: 1, Latinjina, USSR; 2, Muratova, USSR; 3, Kalinjina and Manjina, USSR.

Uneven Bars: 1, Latinjina, USSR; 2, Bosakova, Czechoslovakia; 3, Astakova, USSR.

Balance Beam: 1, Latinjina, USSR; 2, Muratova, USSR; 3, Tanaka, Japan.

Floor Exercise: 1, Bosakova, Czechoslovakia; 2, Latinjina, USSR; 3, Tanaka, Japan.

1962, Prague
TEAM

1, USSR; 2, Czechoslovakia; 3, Japan.
INDIVIDUAL

All-around; 1, Latvnina, USSR; 2, Caslavska, Czechoslovakia; 3, Pervus-china, USSR.

Vault: 1, Caslavska, Czechoslovakia; 2, Latvnina, USSR; 3, Manjina, USSR.

Uneven Bars: 1, Pervuschina, USSR: 2, Bosakova, Czechoslovakia; 3, Latvnina, USSR.

Balance Beam: 1, Bosakova, Czechoslovakia; 2, Latvnina, USSR; 3, Ikeda, Japan and Ducza, Hungary.

Floor Exercise: 1, Latvnina, USSR; 2, Pervuschina, USSR; 3, Caslavska, Czechoslovakia.

1966, Dortmund, West Germany
TEAM

1, Czechoslovakia; 2, USSR; 3, Japan.
INDIVIDUAL

All-around: 1, Caslavska, Czechoslovakia; 2, Kucinskaja, USSR; 3, Ikeda, Japan.

Vault: 1, Caslavska, Czechoslovakia; 2, Zuchold, East Germany; 3, Kucin-skaja, USSR.

Uneven Bars: 1, Kuchinskaja, USSR; 2, Ikeda, Japan; 3, Mitsukuri, Japan.

Balance Beam: 2, Kuchinskaja, USSR; 2, Caslavska, Czechoslovakia; 3, Petrik, USSR.

Floor Exercise: 1, Kuchinskaja, USSR: 2, Caslavska, Czechoslovakia; 3, Druzinina, USSR.

1970, Ljubljana, Yugoslavia
TEAM

1, USSR; 2, East Germany; 3, Czechoslovakia.
INDIVIDUAL

All-around: 1, Turischeva, USSR; 2, Zuchold, East Germany; 3, Voronia, USSR.

Vault: 1, Zuchold, East Germany; 2, Janz, East Germany; 3, Turischeva and Burda, USSR.

Uneven Bars: 1, Janz, East Germany; 2, Turischeva, USSR: 3, Voronia, USSR.

Balance Beam: 1, Zuchold, East Germany; 2, Karazeva, USSR; 3, Petrik and Rigby, USSR and USA.

Floor Exercise: 1, Turischeva, USSR: 2, Voronin, USSR; 3, Schmitt, East Germany.

1974, Varna, Bulgaria
TEAM
1, USSR; 2, East Germany; 3, Hungary.
INDIVIDUAL
All-around: 1, Turischeva, USSR; 2, Korbut, USSR; 3, Hellmann, East Germany.

Vault: 1, Korbut, USSR; 2, Turischeva, USSR: 3, Predlikova, Czechoslovakia.

Uneven Bars: 1, Zinka, East Germany; 2, Korbut, USSR; 3, Turischeva, USSR.

Balance Beam: 1, Turischeva, USSR; 2, Korbut, USSR; 3, Kim, USSR.

Floor Exercise: 1, Turischeva, USSR: 2, Korbut, USSR; 3, Siharulidze and Saadi, USSR.

1978, Strasbourg, France
TEAM
1, USSR; 2, Rumania; 3, East Germany.
INDIVIDUAL
All-around: 1, Moukhina, USSR; 2, Kim, USSR: 3, Shaposhnikova, USSR.

Vault: 1, Kim, USSR; 2, Comaneche, Romania; 3, Kraker, East Germany.

Uneven Bars: 1, Frederick, USA; 2, Moukhina, USSR; 3, Eberle, Rumania.

Balance Beam: 1, Comaneche, Rumania; 2, Moukhina, USSR; 3, Eberle, Rumania.

Floor Exercise: 1, Kim, USSR; 2, Moukhina, USSR; 3, Johnson, USA.

1979, Fort Worth
TEAM
1, Rumania; 2, USSR; 3, East Germany.
INDIVIDUAL
All-around: 1, Kim, USSR; 2, Gnauck, East Germany; 3, Ruhn, Rumania.

Vault: 1, Turner, Rumania; 2, Zakharova, USSR; 3, Kraker, East Germany.

Uneven Bars: 1, Ma, China; 2, Gnauck, East Germany; 3, Eberle, Rumania.

Balance Beam: 1, Cerna, Czechoslovakia; 2, Kim, USSR; 3, Grabolle, Czechoslovakia.

Floor Exercise: 1, Eberle, Rumania; 2, Kim, USSR; 3, Ruhn, Rumania.

1981, Moscow
TEAM
1, USSR; 2, China; 3, East Germany.
INDIVIDUAL
All-around: 1, Bicherova, USSR; 2, Filatova, USSR; 3, Davydova, USSR.

Vault: 2, Gnauck, East Germany; 2, Zakharova, USSR: 3, Kraker, East Germany.

Uneven Bars: 1, Gnauck, East Germany; 2, Ma, China; 3, Davydova and McNamara, USSR and USA.

Balance Beam: 1, Gnauck, East Germany; 2, Wen, China; 3, Talavera, USA.

Floor Exercise: 1, Ilienko, USSR; 2, Davydova, USSR: 3, Grancharova, Bulgaria.

Olympic Games

1952, Helsinki
TEAM
1, USSR; 2, Hungary; 3, Czechoslovakia.
INDIVIDUAL
All-around: 1, Gorokhovskaya, USSR; 2, Borcharova, USSR; 3, Korondi, Hungary.

Vault: 1, Kalinstchu, USSR; 2, Gorokhovskaya, USSR: 3, Minatsheve, USSR.

Uneven Bars: 1, Korondi, Hungary, 2, Gorokhovskaya, USSR; 3, Keleti, Hungary.

Balance Beam: 1, Borcharova, USSR; 2, Gorokhovskaya, USSR; 3, Korondi, Hungary.

Floor Exercise: 1, Keleti, Hungary; 2, Gorokhovskaya, USSR; 3, Korondi, Hungary.

1956, Melbourne
TEAM
1, USSR; 2, Hungary; 3, Rumania.
INDIVIDUAL
All-around: 1, Latvnina, USSR: 2, Keleti, Hungary; 3, Muratova, USSR.

Vault: 1, Latvnina, USSR; 2, Manjina, USSR; 3, Tass, Hungary.

Uneven Bars: 1, Keleti, Hungary; 2, Latvnina, USSR; 3, Muratova, USSR.

Balance Beam: 1, Keleti, Hungary; 2, Manjina, USSR, and Bosakova, Czechoslovakia.

Floor Exercise: 1, Latvnina, USSR, and Keleti, Hungary; 3, Leusteanu, Rumania.

1960, Rome
TEAM
1, USSR; 2, Czechoslovakia; 3, Rumania.
INDIVIDUAL
All-around: 1, Latvnina, USSR; 2, Muratova, USSR; 3, Astakhova, USSR.

Vault: 1, Nicholeava, USSR; 2, Muratova, USSR: 3, Latvnina, USSR.

Uneven Bars: 1, Astakhova, USSR; 2, Latvnina, USSR; 3, Ljukina, USSR.

Balance Beam: 1, Bosakova, Czechoslovakia; 2, Latvnina, USSR; 3, Muratova, USSR.

Floor Exercise: 1, Latvnina, USSR; 2, Astakhova, USSR; 3, Ljukina, USSR.

1964, Tokyo
TEAM
1, USSR; 2, Czechoslovakia; 3, Japan.
INDIVIDUAL
All-around: 1, Caslavska, Czechoslovakia; 2, Latynina, USSR: 3, Astakhova, USSR.

Vault: 1, Caslavska, Czechoslovakia; 2, Latynina, USSR, and Radochia, West Germany

Uneven Bars: 1, Astakhova, USSR; 2, Makray, Hungary; 3, Latynina, USSR.

Balance Beam: Caslavska, Czechoslovakia; 2, Manina, USSR: 3, Latynina, USSR.

Floor Exercise: 1, Latynina, USSR; 2. Astakhova, USSR; 3, Janosi, Hungary.

1968, Mexico City
TEAM
1, USSR; 2, East Germany; 3, Hungary.
INDIVIDUAL
All-around: 1, Turischeva, USSR, and Janz, East Germany; 3, Korbut, USSR.

Vault: 1, Janz, East Germany; 2, Zuchold, East Germany; 3, Turischeva, USSR.

Uneven Bars: 1, Janz, East Germany; 2, Korbut, USSR, and Zuchold, East Germany.

Balance Beam: 1, Korbut, USSR; 2, Lazakovitch, USSR; 3, Janz, East Germany.

Floor Exercise: 1, Korbut, USSR; 2, Turischeva, USSR; 3, Lazakovitch, USSR.

1972, Munich
TEAM
1, USSR; 2, East Germany; 3, Hungary.
INDIVIDUAL
All-around: 1, Turischeva, USSR; 2, Janz, East Germany; 3, Lazakovitch, USSR.

Vault: 1, Janz, East Germany; 2, Zuchold, East Germany; 3, Turischeva, USSR.

Uneven Bars: 1, Janz, East Germany; 2, Korbut, USSR, and Zuchold, East Germany.

Balance Beam: 1, Korbut, USSR; 2, Lazakovitch, USSR; 3, Janz, East Germany.

Floor Exercise: 1, Korbut, USSR; 2, Turischeva, USSR; 3, Lazakovitch, USSR.

1976, Montreal
TEAM

1, USSR; 2, Rumania; 3, East Germany.
INDIVIDUAL

All-around: 1, Comaneche, Rumania; 2, Kim, USSR, and Turischeva, USSR.
Vault: 1, Kim, USSR; 2, Turischeva, USSR, and Dombeck, Rumania.
Uneven Bars: 1, Comaneche, Rumania; 2, Ungureanu, Rumania; 3, Egervari, Hungary.
Balance Beam: 1, Comaneche, Rumania; 2, Korbut, USSR; 3, Ungureanu, Rumania.
Floor Exercise: 1, Kim, USSR; 2, Turischeva, USSR; 3, Comaneche, Rumania.

1980, Moscow
TEAM

1, USSR; 2, Rumania; 3, East Germany.
INDIVIDUAL

All-around: 1, Davydova, USSR; 2, Comaneche, Rumania, and Gnauck, East Germany.
Vault: 1, Shaposhnikova, USSR; 2, Kraker, East Germany; 3, Runn, Rumania.
Uneven Bars: 1, Gnauck, East Germany; 2, Eberle, Rumania; 3, Kraker, East Germany
Balance Beam: 1, Comaneche, Rumania; 2, Davydova, USSR; 3, Shaposhnikova, USSR.
Floor Exercise: 1, Kim, USSR, and Comaneche, Rumania; 3, Shaposhnikova, USSR, and Gnauck, East Germany.

MEN

World Championships

1903, Antwerp
TEAM

1, France; 2, Belgium; 3, Luxemburg.
INDIVIDUAL

All-around: 1, Martinez, France; 2, Lux, France; 3, Wiernick, Belgium
Vault: 1, Dejaeghere, France; 2, Lux, France; 3, Thysen, Holland.
Rings: 1, Martinez, France; 2, Lux, France; 3, Wairavens, Belgium.
Parallel Bars: 1, Martinez, France; 2, Hentges, Luxemburg; 3, Dua, Belgium, and Bordana, Luxemburg.
Horizontal Bar: 1, Martinez, France; 2, Pissie, France; 3, Lecoutre, France, and Van Hulle, Belgium.

1905, Bordeau
TEAM
1, France; 2, Holland; 3, Belgium.
INDIVIDUAL
All-around: 1, Lalue, France; 2, Lavielle, France; 3, Demanet, France.

Vault: 1, Dejaeghere, France; 2. Lalue, France; 3, Lavielle, France.

Parallel Bars: 1, Martinez, France; 2. Lalue, Czechoslovakia; 3, Pausse, France.

Horizontal Bar: 1, Lalue, France; 2, Martinez, France; 3, Demanet and Pausse, France.

1907, Prague
TEAM
1, Czechoslovakia; 2, France; 3, Belgium.
INDIVIDUAL
All-around: 1, Cada, Czechoslovakia; 2, Rolland, France; 3, Erben, Czechoslovakia.

Vault: 1, Erben, Czechoslovakia; 2, Rolland, France; 3, Sal, Czechoslovakia.

Parallel Bars: 1, Lux, France; 2, Cada, Czechoslovakia; 3, Erben, Czechoslovakia, and Segura, France.

Horizontal Bar: 1, Charmoille, France; 2, Erben, Czechoslovakia; 3, Rolland, France.

1909, Luxemburg
TEAM
1, France; 2, Czechoslovakia; 3, Italy.
INDIVIDUAL
All-around: 1, Torres, France; 2, Cada, Czechoslovakia; 3, Coidelle, France

Rings: 1, Romano, Italy; 2. Torres, France; 3, Erben, Czechoslovakia, Manzoncini, Italy, and Zampori, Italy.

Parallel Bars: 1, Martinez, France; 2, Castille, France; 3, Cada, Czechoslovakia, and Torres, France.

Horizontal Bar: 1, Martinez, France; 2, Cada, Czechoslovakia; 3, Erben, Czechoslovakia.

1911, Torino
TEAM
1, Czechoslovakia; 2, France; 3, Italy.
INDIVIDUAL
All-around; 1, Steiner, Czechoslovakia; 2, Cada, Czechoslovakia; 3, Stary, Czechoslovakia, and Svoboda, Czechoslovakia.

Pommel Horse: 1, Palazzi, Italy; 2. Salvi, Italy; 3, Zampori, Italy.

Rings: 1, Steiner, Czechoslovakia; 2, Follacci, France; 3, Bianchi, Italy, and Costa, France.

Parallel Bars: 1, Zampori, Italy; 2. Follacci, France; 3, Steiner, Czechoslovakia, Lecoutre, France, Costa, France, Labieu, France, Salvi, Italy, and Vidmar, Yugoslavia.

Horizontal Bar: 1, Cada, Czechoslovakia; 2, Torres, France; 3, Svoboda, France, and Romano, Italy.

1913, Paris
TEAM
1, Czechoslovakia; 2, France; 3, Italy.
INDIVIDUAL
All-around: 1, Torres, France; 2, Stary, Czechoslovakia; 3, Sykora, Czechoslovakia.

Floor Exercise: 1, Zampori, Italy; 2. Rabic, Yugoslavia; 3, Torres, France.

Pommell Horse: 1, Zampori, Italy; 2, Aubry, France; 3, Palazzi, Italy, and Torres, France.

Rings: 1, Grech, France; 2, Torres, France; 3, Zampori, Italy, and Boni, Italy.

Vault: 1, Stary, Czechoslovakia; 2, Sadoun, France; 3, Palazzi, Italy, and Vidmar, Yugoslavia.

Parallel Bars: 1, Zampori, Italy; 2, Boni, Italy; 3, Hentges, Luxemburg.

Horizontal Bar: 1, Cada, Czechoslovakia; 2, Torres, France; 3, Aubry, France; Demol, Belgium; Palazzi, Italy; and Sykora, Czechoslovakia.

1922, Ljubljana, Yugoslavia
TEAM
1, Czechoslovakia, 2, Yugoslavia; 3, France.
INDIVIDUAL
All-around: 1, Sumi, Yugoslavia; 2, Pechacek, Czechoslovakia; 3, Derganic, Yugoslavia.

Pommel Horse: 1, Klinger, Czechoslovakia; 2, Jindrich, Czechoslovakia, and Stukelj, Yugoslavia; 3, Sumi, Yugoslavia.

Rings: 1, Karasek, Czechoslovakia; 2, Maly, Czechoslovakia, and Stukelj, Yugoslavia; 3, Sumi, Yugoslavia.

Parallel Bars: 1, Stukelj, Yugoslavia; 2, Derganic, Yugoslavia; Jindrich, Czechoslovakia; Klinger, Czechoslovakia; and Simoncic, Yugoslavia; 3, Vidmar, Yugoslavia.

Horizontal Bar: 1, Klinger, Czechoslovakia; 2, Stukelj, Yugoslavia; 3, Sumi, Yugoslavia.

1926, Lyons
TEAM
1, Czechoslovakia; 2, Yugoslavia; 3, France.
INDIVIDUAL
All-around: 1, Sumi, Yugoslavia; 2, Effenberger, Czechoslovakia; 3, Vacha, Czechoslovakia.

Pommel Horse: 1, Karafiat, Czechoslovakia; 2, Gajdos, Czechoslovakia; 3, Vacha, Czechoslovakia.

Rings: 1, Stukelj, Yugoslavia; 2, Vacha, Czechoslovakia; 3, Supcik, Czechoslovakia.

Parallel Bars: 1, Stukelj, Yugoslavia; 2, Primozic, Yugoslavia; 3, Vacha, Czechoslovakia.

1930, Luxemburg
TEAM
1, Czechoslovakia; 2, France; 3, Yugoslavia.
INDIVIDUAL
All-around: 1, Primozic, Yugoslavia; 2, Gajdos, Czechoslavakia; 3, Loffler, Czechoslovakia.

Floor Exercise: 1, Primozic, Yugoslavia; 2, Loffler, Czechoslovakia; 3, Krauss, France.

Pommel Horse: 1, Primozic, Yugoslavia; 2, Sumi, Yugoslavia; 3, Gajdos, Czechoslovakia.

Rings: 1, Loffler, Czechoslovakia; 2, Supcik, Czechoslovakia; 3, Gajdos, Czechoslovakia.

Parallel Bars: 1, Primozic, Yugoslavia; 2, Krauss, France; 3, Vacha, Czechoslovakia.

Horizontal Bar: 1, Pelle, Hungary; 2, Peter, Hungary, 3, Stukelj, Hungary.

1934, Budapest
TEAM
1, Switzerland; 2, Czechoslovakia; 3, Germany.
INDIVIDUAL
All-around: 1, Mack, Switzerland; 2, Neri, Italy; 3, Loffler, Czechoslovakia.

Floor Exercise: 1, Miez, Switzerland; 2, Mack, Switzerland; 3, Kortsch, Germany.

Pommel Horse: 1, Mack, Switzerland; 2, Steinemann, Switzerland; 3, Sladek, Czechoslovakia.

Rings: 1, Hudek, Czechoslovakia; 2, Mack, Switzerland; 3, Logelin, Luxemburg, and Kolinger, Czechoslovakia.

Vault: 1, Mack, Switzerland; 2. Steinemann, Switzerland; 3, Neri, Italy.

Parallel Bars: 1, Mack, Switzerland; 2, Walter, Switzerland; 3, Bach, Switzerland.

Horizontal Bar: 1, Winter, Germany; 2, Sandrock, Germany; 3, Miez, Switzerland.

1938, Prague
TEAM
1, Czechoslovakia; 2, Switzerland; 3, Yugoslavia.
INDIVIDUAL
All-around: 1, Gadjdos, Czechoslovakia; 2, Sladek, Czechoslovakia; 3, Mack, Switzerland.

Floor Exercise: 1, Gadjdos, Czechoslovakia; 2, Mack, Switzerland; 3, Hudec, Czechoslovakia.

Pommel Horse: 1, Reusch, Switzerland; 2, Petracek, Czechoslovakia; 3, Schurmann, Switzerland.

Rings: 1, Hudec, Czechoslovakia; 2, Reusch, Switzerland; 3, Petracek, Czechoslovakia.

Vault: 1, Mack, Switzerland; 2, Beck, Switzerland; 3, Nagelin, Switzerland.

Parallel Bars: 1, Reusch, Switzerland; 2, Hudec, Czechoslovakia; 3, Primozic, Yugoslavia.

Horizontal Bar: 1, Reusch, Switzerland; 2, Hudec, Czechoslovakia; 3, Beck, Switzerland.

1950, Basel
TEAM
1, Switzerland; 2, Finland; 3, France.
INDIVIDUAL
All-around: 1, Lehmann, Switzerland; 2, Adatte, Switzerland; 3, Rowe, Finland.

Floor Exercise: 1, Stalder, Switzerland; 2, Gebendinger, Switzerland; 3, Dot, France.

Pommel Horse: 1, Stalder, Switzerland; 2, Adatte, Switzerland; 3, Lehmann, Switzerland.

Rings: 1, Lehmann, Switzerland; 2, Rowe, Finland; 3, Eugster, Switzerland.

Vault: 1, Gebendinger, Switzerland; 2, Rowe, Finland; 3, Lehmann, Switzerland.

Parallel Bars: 1, Eugster, Switzerland; 2, Rowe, Finland; 3, Dot, France.

Horizontal Bar: 1, Aaltonen, Finland; 2, Huhtanen, Finland; 3, Lehmann and Stalder, Switzerland.

1954, Rome
TEAM
1, USSR; 2, Japan; 3, Switzerland.
INDIVIDUAL
All-around: 1, Muratov, USSR; 2, Chukarin, USSR; 3, Saginjan, USSR.

Floor Exercise: 1, Muratov, USSR; 2, Takemoto, Japan; 3, Torreson, Sweden.

Pommel Horse: 1, Saginjan, USSR; 2, Stalder, Switzerland; 3, Chukarin, USSR.

Rings: 1, Azarian, USSR; 2, Korolkov, USSR; 3, Muratov, USSR.

Vault: 1, Sotornik, USSR: 2, Bantz, West Germany; 3, Djaiani, USSR.

Parallel Bars: 1, Chukarin, USSR; 2, Stalder, Switzerland; 3, Takemoto, Japan; Engster, Switzerland; and Bantz, West Germany.

Horizontal Bar: 1, Muratov, USSR; 2, Bantz, West Germany, and Shaklin, USSR: 3, Retti, Hungary.

1958, Moscow
TEAM

1, USSR; 2, Japan; 3, Czechoslovakia.

INDIVIDUAL

All-around: 1, Shaklin, USSR; 2, Ono, Japan; 3, Titov, USSR.

Floor Exercise: 1, Takemoto, Japan; 2, Ono, Japan; 3, Titov, USSR.

Pommel Horse: 1, Shaklin, USSR; 2, Stolbov, USSR; Cerar, Yugoslavia.

Rings: 1, Azarian, USSR; 2, Aihara, Japan; 3, Titov, USSR.

Vault: 1, Titov, USSR: 2, Takemoto, Japan; 3, Ono, Japan.

Parallel Bars: 1, Shaklin, USSR; 2, Ono, Japan; 3, Stolbov, USSR.

Horizontal Bar: 1, Shaklin, USSR; 2, Azarian, USSR; 3, Titov, USSR, and Takemoto, Japan.

1962, Prague
TEAM

1, Japan; 2, USSR; 3, Czechoslovakia.

INDIVIDUAL

All-around: 1, Titov, USSR; 2, Endo, Japan; 3, Shaklin, USSR.

Floor Exercise: 1, Aihara, Japan; 2, Endo, Japan; 3, Menichelli, Italy.

Pommel Horse: 1, Cerar, Yugoslavia; 2, Shaklin, USSR; 3, Mitsukuri, Japan, and Yu Lieh, China.

Rings: 1, Titov, USSR; 2, Endo, Japan; 3, Shaklin, USSR.

Vault: 1, Krbeck, Czechoslovakia; 2, Yamashita, Japan; 3, Shaklin, USSR, and Endo, Japan.

Parallel Bars: 1, Cerar, Czechoslovakia; 2, Shaklin, USSR; 3, Endo, Japan.

Horizontal Bar: 1, Ono, Japan; 2, Endo, Japan; 3, Stolbov, USSR.

1966, Dortmund, West Germany
TEAM

1, Japan; 2, USSR; 3, East Germany.

INDIVIDUAL

All-around: 1, Voronin, USSR; 2, Tsurumi, Japan; 3, Nakayama, Japan.

Floor Exercise: 1, Nakayama, Japan; 2, Endo, Japan; 3, Menichelli, Italy.
Pommel Horse: 1, Cerar, Yugoslavia; 2, Voronin, USSR; 3, Kato, Japan.
Rings: 1, Voronin, USSR; 2, Nakayama, Japan; 3, Menichelli, Italy.
Vault: 1, Matsuda, Japan; 2, Kato, Japan; 3, Nakayama, Japan.
Parallel Bars: 1, Diamidov, USSR; 2, Voronin, USSR; 3, Cerar, Yugoslavia.
Horizontal Bar: 1, Nakayama, Japan; 2, Endo, Japan; 3, Mitsukuri, Japan.

1970, Ljubljana, Yugoslavia
TEAM

1, Japan; 2, USSR; 3, East Germany.

INDIVIDUAL

All-around: 1, Kenmotsu, Japan; 2, Tsukahara, Japan; 3, Nakayama, Japan.
Floor Exercise: 1, Nakayama, Japan; 2, Kenmotsu, Japan; 3, Kato, Japan.
Pommel Horse: 1, Cerar, Yugoslavia; 2, Kenmotsu, Japan; 3, Klimenko,
USSR.
Rings: 1, Nakayama, Japan; 2, Tsukahara, Japan; 3, Voronin, USSR.
Vault: 1, Tsukahara, Japan; 2, Klimenko, USSR; 3, Kato, Japan.
Parallel Bars: 1, Nakayama, Japan; 2, Kenmotsu, Japan; 3, Voronin, USSR.
Horizontal Bar: 1, Kenmotsu, Japan; 2, Nakayama, Japan; 3, Hayata, Japan,
and Koste, East Germany.

1974, Varna, Bulgaria
TEAM

1, Japan; 2, USSR; 3, East Germany.

INDIVIDUAL

All-around; 1, Kasamatsu, Japan; 2, Andrianov, USSR; 3, Kenmotsu, Japan.
Floor Exercise: 1, Kasamatsu, Japan; 2, Kajiyama, Japan; 3, Keranov,
Bulgaria.
Pommel Horse: 1, Magyar, Hungary; 2, Andrianov, USSR; 3, Kenmotsu,
Japan.
Rings: 1, Andrianov, USSR: 2, Grecu, Romania; 3, Szajna, Poland.
Vault: 1, Kasamatsu, Japan; 2, Andrianov, USSR; 3, Kajiyama, Japan.
Parallel Bars: 1, Kenmotsu, Japan; 2, Andrianov, USSR; 3, Marchenko,
USSR.
Horizontal Bar: 1, Gienger, West Germany; 2, Thune, East Germany; 3,
Kenmotsu, Japan, and Szajna, Poland.

1978, Strasbourg, France
TEAM

1, Japan; 2, USSR; 3, East Germany.

INDIVIDUAL

All-around: 1, Andrianov, USSR; 2, Kenmotsu, Japan; 3, Ditiatin, USSR.
Floor Exercise: 1, Thomas, USA; 2, Kasamatsu, Japan; 3, Ditiatin, USSR.

Pommel Horse: 1, Magyar, Hungary; 2, Gienger, West Germany; 3, Deltchev, Bulgaria.

Rings: 1, Andrianov, USSR; 2, Ditiatin, USSR; 3, Grecu, Romania.

Vault: 1, Shimizu, Japan; 2, Andrianov, USSR: 3, Barthel, East Germany.

Parallel Bars: 1, Kenmotsu, Japan; 2, Andrianov, USSR: 3, Kajiyama, Japan.

Horizontal Bar: 1, Kasamatsu, Japan; 2, Gienger, West Germany; 3, Deltchev, Bulgaria, and Krysin, USSR.

1979, Fort Worth
TEAM

1, USSR; 2, Japan; 3, USA.

INDIVIDUAL

All-around: 1, Ditiatin, USSR; 2, Thomas, USA; 3, Tkachev, USSR.

Floor Exercise: 1, Thomas, USA; 2, Bruckner, East Germany; 3, Tkachev, USSR.

Pommel Horse: l, Magyar, Hungary; 2, Thomas USA; 3, Gushiken, Japan.

Rings: 1, Ditiatin, USSR: 2, Grecu, Romania; 3, Tkachev, USSR.

Vault; 1, Ditiatin, USSR: 2, Andrianov, USSR; 3, Conner, USA, and Barthel, East Germany.

Parallel Bars: 1, Conner, USA; 2, Thomas, USA; 3, Ditiatin, USSR.

Horizontal Bar: 1, Thomas USA; 2, Tkachev, USSR; 3, Ditiatin, USSR.

1981, Moscow
TEAM

1, USSR; 2, Japan; 3, China.

INDIVIDUAL

All-around; 1, Korolev, USSR; 2, Makuts, USSR; 3, Gushiken, Japan.

Floor Exercise: 1, Korolev, USSR; 2, Li, China; 3, Gushiken, Japan.

Pommel Horse: 1, Nikolay, East Germany; 2, Li, China; 3, Korolev, USSR.

Rings: 1. Ditiatin, USSR; 2. Juan, China; 3, Makuts, USSR.

Vault: 1, Herman, East Germany; 2, Akapian, USSR; 3, Makuta, USSR.

Parallel Bars: 1. Gushiken, Japan; 2, Ditiatin, USSR; 3, Kajitani, Japan.

Horizontal Bar: 1, Tkachev, USSR; 2, Akapian, USSR; 3, Gienger, West Germany.

Olympic Games 1948-1980

1948, London
TEAM

1, Finland; 2, Switzerland; 3, Hungary.

INDIVIDUAL

All-around: 1, Huhtanen, Finland; 2, Lehmann, Switzerland; 3, Aaltonen, Finland.

Floor Exercise: 1, Pataki, Hungary; 2, Magyorossi, Hungary; 3, Ruzicka, Czechoslovakia.

Pommel Horse: 1, Huhtanen, Finland; 2, Aaltonen, Finland; 3, Savolainen, Finland.

Rings: 1, Frei, Switzerland; 2, Reutsch, Switzerland; 3, Ruzicka, Czechoslovakia.

Vault: 1, Aaltonen, Finland; 2, Rove, Finland; 3, Pataki, Hungary.

Parallel Bars: 1, Reutsch, Switzerland; 2, Huhtanen, Finland; 3, Kipfer, Switzerland.

Horizontal Bar: 1, Stalder, Switzerland; 2, Lehmann, Switzerland; 3, Huhtanen, Finland.

1952, Helsinki
TEAM

1, USSR; 2, Switzerland; 3, Finland

INDIVIDUAL

All-around: 1, Shukarin, USSR; 2, Chaquinian, USSR; 3, Stalder, Switzerland.

Floor Exercise: 1, Thoresson, Sweden; 2, Uesado, Japan, and Jokiel, Poland.

Pommel Horse: 1, Shukarin, USSR; 2, Chaquinian, USSR, and Korolkov, USSR.

Rings: 1, Chaquinian, USSR; 2, Shukarin, USSR; 3, Eugster, Switzerland.

Vault: 1, Shukarin, USSR; 2, Takemoto, Japan; 3, Ono, Japan and Uesako, Japan.

Parallel Bars: 1, Eugster, Switzerland; 2, Shukarin, USSR; 3, Stalder, Switzerland.

Horizontal Bar: 1, Gunthard, Switzerland; 2, Stalder, Switzerland, and Schwarzmann, W. Germany.

1956, Melbourne
TEAM

1, USSR; 2, Japan; 3, Finland.

INDIVIDUAL

All-around: 1, Shukarin, USSR; 2, Ono, Japan; 3, Titov, USSR.

Floor Exercise: 1, Mouratov, USSR; Shukarin, USSR, and Thoresson, Sweden, and Aihara, Japan.

Pommel Horse: 1, Shaklin, USSR; 2, Ono, Japan; 3, Shukarin, USSR.

Rings: 1, Azarian, USSR; 2, Mouratov, USSR; 3, Kubota, Japan, and Takemoto, Japan.

Vault: 1, Bantz, W. Germany, and Mouratov, USSR; 3, Titov, USSR.

Parallel Bars: 1, Shaklin, USSR; 2, Kubota, Japan; 3, Takemoto, Japan, and Ono, Japan.

Horizontal Bar: 1, Ono, Japan; 2, Takemoto, Japan; 3, Shaklin, USSR.

1964, Tokyo
TEAM

1, Japan; 2, USSR; 3, East Germany.

INDIVIDUAL

All-around: 1, Endo, Japan; 2, Tsurumi, Japan, and Shaklin, USSR, and Lisitky, USSR.

Floor Exercise: 1, Menichelli, Italy; 2, Lisitsky, USSR; 3, Endo, Japan.

Pommel Horse: 1, Cerar, Yugoslavia; 2, Tsurumi, Japan; 3, Tsapenko, USSR.

Rings: 1, Hayata, Japan; 2, Menichelli, Italy; 3, Shaklin, USSR.

Vault: 1, Yamashita, Japan; 2, Lisitsky, USSR; 3, Rantakari, Finland.

Parallel Bars: 1, Endo, Japan; 2, Tsurumi, Japan; 3, Menichelli, Italy.

Horizontal Bar: 1, Shaklin, USSR; 2, Titov, USSR; 3, Cerar, Yugoslavia.

1968, Mexico City
TEAM

1, Japan; 2, USSR; 3, East Germany.

INDIVIDUAL

All-around: 1, Kato, Japan; 2, Voronin, USSR; 3, Nakayama, Japan.

Floor Exercise: 1, Kato, Japan; 2, Nakayama, Japan; 3, Kasamatsu, Japan.

Pommel Horse: 1, Cerar, Yugoslavia; 2, Laiho, Finland; 3, Voronin, USSR.

Rings: 1, Nakayama, Japan; 2, Voronin, USSR; 3, Kato, Japan.

Vault: 1, Voronin, USSR; 2, Endo, Japan; 3, Diamidov, USSR.

Parallel Bars: 1, Nakayama, Japan; 2, Voronin, USSR; 3, Klimenko, USSR.

Horizontal Bar: 1, Voronin, USSR, and Nakayama, Japan; 3, Kenmotsu, Japan.

1972, Munich
TEAM

1, Japan; 2, USSR; 3, East Germany.

INDIVIDUAL

All-around: 1, Kato, Japan; 2, Kenmotsu, Japan; 3, Kasamatsu, Japan.

Floor Exercise: 1, Andrianov, USSR; 2, Nakayama, Japan; 3, Kasamatsu, Japan.

Pommel Horse: 1, Klimenko, USSR; 2, Kato, Japan; 3, Kenmotsu, Japan.

Rings: 1, Nakayama, Japan; 2, Voronin, USSR; 3, Tsukahara, Japan.

Vault: 1, Koste, East Germany; 2, Klimenko, USSR; 3, Andrianov, USSR.

Parallel Bars: 1, Kata, Japan; 2, Kasamatsu, Japan; 3, Kenmotsu, Japan.
Horizontal Bar: 1, Tsukahara, Japan; 2, Kato, Japan; 3, Kasamatsu, Japan.

1976, Montreal
TEAM
1, Japan; 2, USSR; 3, East Germany.
INDIVIDUAL
All-around: 1, Andrianov, USSR; 2, Kato, Japan; 3, Tsukahara, Japan.
Floor Exercise: 1, Andrianov, USSR; 2, Marchenko, USSR; 3, Korman, USA.
Pommel Horse: 1, Magyar, Hungary; 2, Kenmotsu, Japan; 3, Andrianov,
USSR, and Nikolai, East Germany.
Rings: 1, Andrianov, USSR; 2, Ditiatin, USSR; 3, Grecu, Romania.
Vault: 1, Andrianov, USSR; 2, Tsukahara, Japan; 3, Kajiyama, Japan.
Parallel Bars: 1, Kato, Japan; 2, Andrianov, USSR; 3, Tsukahara, Japan.
Horizontal Bar: 1, Tsukahara, Japan; 2, Kenmotsu, Japan; 3, Boerio, France,
and Gienger, West Germany.

1980, Moscow
TEAM
1, USSR; 2, East Germany; 3, Hungary.
INDIVIDUAL
All-around: 1, Ditiatin, USSR; 2, Andrianov, USSR; 3, Deltchev, Bulgaria.
Floor Exercise: 1, Bruckner, East Germany; 2, Andrianov, USSR; 3, Ditiatin,
USSR.
Pommel Horse: 1, Magyar, Hungary; 2, Ditiatin, USSR; 3, Nikolay, East
Germany.
Rings: 1, Ditiatin, USSR; 2, Tkatchev, USSR; 3, Tabak, Czechoslovakia.
Vault: 1, Ditiatin, USSR; 2, Bruckner, East Germany; 3, Andrianov, USSR.
Parallel Bars: 1, Tkatchev, USSR; 2, Ditiatin, USSR; 3, Bruckner, East
Germany.
Horizontal Bar: 1, Deltchev, Bulgaria; 2, Ditiatin, USSR; 3, Andrianov,
USSR.

TOP GYMNASTICS TRAINING PROGRAMS IN THE UNITED STATES

The following programs have been selected because, in the opinion of Bill Sands, they have produced many high-ranking gymnasts and/or exhibit a healthy attitude towards gymnastics.

GYMNASTICS CLUBS

Almaden Valley Gymnastics Club
Coach Jim Turpin — Women
19600 Almaden Rd.
San Jose, California 95120

Arizona Twisters
Coach Roe Kreutzer — Women
8232 E. Vista Dr.
Scottsdale, Arizona 85253

Atlanta School of Gymnastics
Coach Tom and Bunny Cook — Men
   and Women
1804 Montreal Ct.
Tucker, Georgia 30084

Berks Gymnastics Academy
Coach Tom McCarthy — Women
1405 Penn Ave
Wyomissing, Pennsylvania 19610

Flips Olympic Academy
Coach Nancy Roach and Al Lansdon—
   Women
1510 The Strand
Reno, Nevada 89503

Grossfelds American Gold — Women
229 Orange Ave.
Milford, Connecticut 06460

Gym-Dandys
Coach Danny Warbutton — Women
1620 Jefferson Ave.
Washington, Pennsylvania 15031

GymnastiCenter
Coach Yoichi Tomita — Men
PO Box 43172
Tucson, Arizona 85732

Gymnastics Academy of Cleveland
Coach Skip Eckert — Women
5400 W. 161 St.
Brookpark, Ohio 44142

Gymnastics Oklahoma
Coach Paul Ziert — Men and Women
7420 N. Broadway Extension
Oklahoma City, Oklahoma 73116

Gymnastics Olympica
Coach Fritz Reiter — Women
7735 Haskell Ave.
Van Nuys, California 91406

Jonathan's Living Seagulls
Coach John Tobler — Women
11121 Greenbriar Rd.
Minnetonka, Minnesota 55343

Karolyi's World Gymnastics, Inc.
Coach Bella and Marta Karolyi —
  Women
17203 Bamwood
Houston, Texas 77090

Los Altos Twisters
Coach Kim and Nancy Kludt —
  Women
2639a Terminal Blvd.
Mountain View, California 94043

Marvateens
Coach Gary Anderson — Women
5636 Randolph Rd.
Rockville, Maryland 20853

National Academy of Artistic
  Gymnastics
Coach Dick Mulvihill — Women
Coach Mizo Mizoguchi — Men
148 West 12th St.
Eugene, Oregon 97401

Parkettes
Coach Bill and Donna Strauss - Women
10 Juniper Rd. A.O.
Macungie, Pennsylvania 18062

Puget Sound School of Gymnastics
Coach Brad Loan — Women
6701 S. Adams St.
Tacoma, Washington 98409

SCATS
Coach Don Peters — Women
5822 Research Dr.
Huntington Beach, California 92649

UNIVERSITY PROGRAMS

Arizona State University
Coach Don Robinson — Men
Coach John Spini — Women
Athletic Department
Tempe, Arizona 85281

California State University Fullerton
Coach Dick Wolfe — Men
Coach Lynn Rogers — Women
Athletic Department
Fullerton, California 92634

East Stroudsburg State College
Coach Bruno Klaus — Men
Route 3, Box 3597
Stroudsburg, Pennsylvania 18360

Indiana State University
Coach Grete Trieber — Women
Athletic Department
Terre Haute, Indiana 47809

Iowa State University
Coach Ed Gagnier — Men
Athletic Department
Ames, Iowa 50011

Northern Illinois University
Coach Chuck Ehrlich — Men
Athletic Department
Dekalb, Illinois 60115

Ohio State University
Athletic Department
Columbus, Ohio 43210

Pennsylvania State University
Coach Karl Schwenzfier — Men
Coach Judy Avener — Women
113 White Building
University Park, Pennsylvania 16802

Southern Connecticut State College
Coach Abe Grossfeld — Men
Athletic Department
New Haven, Connecticut 06515

Southern Illinois University
Coach Bill Meade — Men
Coach Herb Vogel — Women
Athletic Department
Carbondale, Illinois 62901

Temple University
Coach Fred Turoff — Men
Athletic Department
Philadelphia, Pennsylvania 19122

University of California — Berkeley
Coach Hal Frey — Men
Coach Diane Dunbar — Women
Athletic Department
Berkeley, California 94720

University of California — Los Angeles
Coach Makoto Sakamoto and Art
    Shurlock — Men
Coach Jerry Tomlinson — Women
405 Hilgard Ave.
Los Angeles, California 90024

University of Illinois
Coach Yoshi Hayasaki — Men
2511 Hathaway Dr.
Champaign, Illinois 61820

University of Illinois — Chicago Circle
    Campus
Coach Clarence Johnson
Chicago Circle
Chicago, Illinois 60680

University of Iowa
Athletic Department
Iowa City, Iowa 52242

University of Michigan
Athletic Department
Ann Arbor, Michigan 48109

University of Minnesota
Coach Fred Roethlisberger — Men
Athletic Department
Minneapolis, Minnesota 55455

University of Nebraska
Coach Francis Allen and Jim Howard
    — Men
Athletic Department
Lincoln, Nebraska 68583

University of Oklahoma
Coach Paul Ziert — Men
Athletic Department
Norman, Oklahoma 73019

University of Oregon
Coach Ron Ludwig — Women
Athletic Department
Eugene, Oregon 97403

University of Southern California
Coach Zen Kinolik — Women
Heritage Hall
Los Angeles, California 90007

University of Utah
Coach Greg Marsden — Women
Athletic Department
Salt Lake City, Utah 84112

University of Washington
Coach Bob Ito — Women
Athletic Department
Seattle, Washington 98195

University of Wisconsin
Coach Mark Pflughoeft — Men
Athletic Department
Madison, Wisconsin 53706

University of Wisconsin — Oshkosh
Coach Ken Allen — Men
Kolf Sports Center
Oshkosh, Wisconsin 54901

Western Michigan University
Coach Fred Orlofsky — Men
6261 N. 8th St.
Kalamazoo, Michigan 49003

SUMMER CAMPS AND SPECIAL PROGRAMS

Camp Tsukara
Summer Camp — Boys and Girls
Contact: Jerry Fontana
Tsukara
3909 Rugen Rd. No. 1
Glenview, Illinois 60025

International Gymnastics Training
Camp
Summer Camp — Boys and Girls
Contact: International Gymnastics
Camp
R. D. 3, Box 3597B
Stroudsburg, Pennsylvania 18360

The Karolyi's Gymnastics World Camps
Summer Camp — Women Only
Contact: Karolyi's Gymnastics World
Camps
17203 Bamwood
Houston, Texas 77090

The National Academy Gymnastics
Camp
Summer Camp — Women Only
Contact: National Academy of Artistic
Gymnastics
148 West 12th Street
Eugene, Oregon 97401

The National Gymnastics Training
Centre
Summer Camp — Boys and Girls
Huguenot, New York 12746
Contact: Call (914) 856-4382

Parkette Gymnastics Camp
Summer Camp — Boys and Girls
Contact: Bill Strauss
Parkettes
401 Lawrence Str.
Allentown, Pennsylvania 18102

United States Gymnastics Training
Center
Summer Camp — Boys and Girls
Contact: USGTC
Box 1090
Cotuit, Massachusetts 02635

Woodward Gymnastics Camp
Summer Camp — Boys and Girls
Contact: Woodward Gymnastics Camp
Woodward, Pennsylvania 16882

MAJOR GYMNASTICS ASSOCIATIONS

AAU
3400 W. 86th St.
Indianapolis, Indiana 46268
(317) 297-2900

The AAU is responsible for some competitions and its own series of national championships.

Canadian Gymnastics Federation
11th Floor 333 River Road
Vanier, Ontario, Canada
K118B9
(416) 491-5050

The CGF is the Canadian counterpart to our USGF.

Federation of International Gymnastics
M. Max Bangerter, Secretary General
Juraweg 12
3250 Lyss
Switzerland

The FIG is the international governing body for gymnastics. The FIG is run by various committees so that information about particular matters might better be approached through the appropriate committees. These committees can be identified through the USGF as the members are changeable and the USGF must keep up to date on these matters.

International Gymnast Magazine
PO Box 110
Santa Monica, California 90406

The IG is the oldest gymnastics magazine of national and international scope in the United States.

International Trampoline Technical
  Committee
PO Box 4, 0672 USL
Lafayette, Louisiana 70504

The National Association of
Intercollegiate Athletics
1221 Baltimore
Kansas City, Missouri 64105
(816) 842-5050
Smaller colleges.

The National Collegiate Athletic
Association
PO Box 1906
Shawnee Mission, Kansas 66222
(913) 384-3220
The NCAA is responsible for most gymnastics in the higher level universities for both men and women.

National Federation of High Schools
11724 Plaza Circle
Kansas City, Missouri 64195
This organization is responsible for governing some state high school athletic programs.

National High School Coaches
Association
3423 E. Silver Spring
Ocala, Florida 32670

Olympic Training Center
Olympic House
United States Olympic Committee
Colorado Springs, Colorado 80909

Special Olympics
1701 K St. NW, No. 203
Washington, D.C. 20006
(202) 331-1346
The Special Olympics offers gym-nastics competitions at some levels for the disabled or handicapped athlete.

United States Association of
Independent Gymnastics Clubs
Ed Knepper, Director
235 Pinehurst Rd.
Wilmington, Delaware 19803
(302) 656-3715
The USAIGC is a supporter and developer of independent gymnastics clubs in the United States.

United States Gymnastics Federation
PO Box 1977
Indianapolis, Indiana 46204
(317) 638-8743
The USGF is the national governing body for the U.S. in amateur gymnastics. Responsible for coordinating and ruling most of the gymnastics activities in this country.

The other associations mentioned in this book are part of the USGF and can be reached through the USGF national office. Since the USGF is governed largely by committees and these committees often change memberships one is best able to get to the information by contacting the USGF first.

GLOSSARY

Afterflight

The gymnast's flight from the horse to the landing.

Barani

A front somersault with a half twist.

Beat the bar

Tapping the bar with the thighs during a hanging skill or striking the bar with the hips and abdomen with a whipping action, performed with the hands grasping the high bar.

Cast

The first skill learned on the horizontal bar and the uneven bars. While in a front support position, the gymnast swings the legs forward and then backward with enough force that the hips leave the bar and the gymnast is supported only by the hands.

Compulsory

A prescribed exercise for men or women in each event. It must be performed as written in a text provided by the governing body that is officiating the competition. The compulsory exercise is scored from 10.00 points, and thus forms half of the gymnast's all-around score.

Core score

The score sometimes referred to as the base score, it is derived by averaging the two middle scores of the four judges. The core score is averaged with a superior judge's score if there is an irreconcilable problem of agreeing on the score to be awarded to the gymnast.

Crash mat

The large, soft mat, usually made of foam rubber and covered with vinyl or other plastic material, used to cushion landings and falls.

Cross grip

The manner of holding the bar in which the arms are crossed and in an overgrip, so that the left hand is on the right side of the bar and the right hand on the left side. This grip is used to turn a gymnast as he or she swings since the grip will "unwind" and serve to turn the gymnast about the long axis of the body.

Croupe

The hind quarters of a pommel horse. When facing the horse's side, the croupe is to the left. Historically, the croupe resembled a real horse's hind-quarters; the early version of gymnastics horses had tails and a raised end for the neck. In men's gymnastics, the croupe always refers to the near end of the horse as the gymnast approaches the horse from his run in long horse vaulting.

Cubital grip

A variation on the grip in which the gymnast not only has his arms and hands twisted but turns his wrists out as he passes over the bar so that he has support.

Deduction

The gymnast usually begins with a 10.00 score, and the judges then take away points from this score to arrive at the final score—based on the number and size of the errors made by the gymnast. The points taken away from the gymnast are the deductions.

Dismount

The last skill or series of skills in the routine.

Elgrip

Also called the Eagle grip. This is an unusual way of gripping the bar and requires flexible shoulders. When a swimmer does the backstroke, during the water contact phase of his armswing his hands and arms strike the water in an elgrip position.

Elite level

The term traditionally reserved for the highest level of gymnastics per-former in our country. The U.S. Olympic and World teams are selected from the Elite level.

English position

The handstand position in which the hands are very close together rather than in line with the shoulders. The English position is performed on the balance beam and the men's parallel bars.

Family

Skill families and vault families are skills or tricks that have similar roots in a movement pattern. For example, all somersaulting handsprings belong in the same family on the vault, whether there is additional twist or more than one somersault.

Flip-flop

A slang term for somersault or one rotation of the body while unsupported.

Foam pit

Large areas of torn-up pieces of foam which are fluffy and soft so that the gymnast can fall into the pit with little fear of injury.

Full in

The full in is a shortened phrase for a "full in to back somersault out" double somersault. This refers to a double backward somersault with a full twist about the long axis of the gymnast during the first somersault.

Full out

The full out is a shortened phrase for a "back somersault in to full out" double somersault. This refers to a double somersault with a full twist in the second somersault.

Giant swing

The giant swing is performed in both men's and women's events. It consists of swinging about the hands in a fully or near fully stretched body position for one complete revolution about the bar or rings.

Handspring

Handsprings are done forward over the vault horse, and either forward or backward in tumbling. They consist of a quick jump or kick through a handstand with a quick push from the hands to arrive on the feet again. The name comes from the "springing" action provided by the hands.

Half in - half out

A double somersault with a half twist in the first somersault and a half twist in the second somersault.

Handspring full

A shortened phrase for the handspring vault with a full twist. The twist is performed during the afterflight phase and has been a compulsory vault for some time.

Hurdle

The preparatory step for some kind of take-off. The hurdle in tumbling is a short hop that allows the gymnast to prepare for the handspring or round-off. The hurdle in the vault allows the gymnast to go from alternate stepping in the run to a feet-together take-off position on the board.

Hanging event
Traditionally, the rings and the horizontal bar.

Inquiry
A format for questioning the score awarded to a female gymnast. The coach or delegation leader in international competition can file an inquiry with the jury of appeals to go over the gymnast's routine and determine if any mistakes were made in awarding the score.

Layout
The position in which the gymnast maintains a straight body through the skill. The legs, hips, and body should all be in alignment.

Limber
Similar to a walkover, except that the gymnast performs the entire skill with the legs together. There are forward and backward versions, and the gymnast must have considerable flexibility to perform them.

Lunge
A position used before some tumbling skills prior to take-off. The gymnast has one leg in front, with a bent knee and the foot on the floor. The other leg is behind, with a straight knee and the foot on the floor. The torso is held upright and stretched with arms overhead.

Mount
The first skill or series of skills executed in a routine.

Neck
The portion of the horse to the right as the gymnast faces the horse from the side. In men's vaulting, the neck always refers to the far end of the horse as the gymnast makes his approach.

Olympic order
The traditional order of competition for the individual events. The men compete following the order of floor exercise, pommel horse, still rings, long horse vault, parallel bars, and horizontal bar. The women compete their Olympic order with the vault, uneven bars, balance beam, and finally the floor exercise.

One-arm giant
In this new type of giant swing, the gymnast performs revolutions about the horizontal bar holding onto it with only one hand throughout the complete revolution.

Overgrip

The manner of holding the bar or rings with the hands in the most comfortable and natural position, i.e., the normal chin-up grip with the backs of the hands facing the gymnast.

Pike

The position in which the gymnast is bent forward at the hips but holds his legs and torso straight.

Planche

A strength and balance skill in which the gymnast's body is parallel to the floor, supported with straight arms and hands on the apparatus or the floor.

Preflight

The portion of the men's or women's vault during which the gymnast is airborne between the vaulting board and the horse.

Press

A slow movement to a handstand, as opposed to a swinging or diving movement. The press requires strength and is usually done to show slow, elegant movement.

Protest

A format for questioning the score awarded to a male gymnast.

Puck position

A cross between a tuck and a pike position. The gymnast uses this position to perform multiple somersaulting skills with twists. The puck looks like an open tuck.

Routine

The planned order of elements that make up a gymnast's exercise.

Run

Refers to the tumbling run. The tumbling run is a series of tumbling skills done in succession—without hesitation—and covering several feet or perhaps the entire diagonal of the mat.

Saddle

The middle portion of the horse or the area between the pommels.

Snap-down

The portion of a back handspring or Tsukahara vault that consists of a violent hip pike combined with a forceful push from the shoulders. The snap-down serves to rotate the gymnast to his or her feet from a handstand, or to somersault the gymnast.

Spotting belt

A leather or nylon belt worn about the waist of the gymnast when learning a skill. Ropes are attached to the belt and then held by teachers, or are strung from pulleys in the ceiling. The teachers holding the ropes follow the gymnast through a skill with just enough tension on the ropes to aid but not interfere with the gymnast's movements. The ropes allow the teacher to pull up on the gymnast during a dangerous point of the skill to prevent or soften a fall.

Step-out

The step-out is a landing position from a somersault in which the gymnast lands on one foot at a time rather than with both feet at the same time.

Streulli

A skill performed on the parallel bars in which a gymnast does a backward roll on his upper arms and extends to a handstand during the upswing phase.

"Stuck" landing

The gymnast's landings in floor exercise and dismounts should occur without stumbling, and the gymnast should make no extra movements upon foot contact with the floor, hence the term "stuck."

Stutz

A skill on the parallel bars in which the gymnast swings from a handstand downward and forward to upward. On the upward swing the gymnast performs a half-turn to land in support.

Support

A position in which the gymnast supports the body on the hands with straight arms.

Support event

Support events in men's gymnastics are traditionally the pommel horse and the parallel bars.

Symmetry

Refers to the alignment and position of body parts relative to each other. The symmetry of the body is maintained if both left and right sides perform movements in exactly the same format. Symmetry is lost when the left and right side do not move in the same pattern.

Tinsica

A walkover done with one hand in front of the other.

Tuck

The tumbling position in which the knees are drawn to the chest and grasped by the gymnast's arms. The back is rounded and the head is down.

Tumbling pass

A line or series of skills performed by starting with a running approach and then performing several skills in succession, followed by an ending skill which terminates the series.

Twist

Twisting movements consist of turns about the long axis of the body. Twisting skills are usually described by the number of times the gymnast turns, i.e., full, double, triple, one and a half, etc.

Walkover

The walkover is performed either forward or backward and is largely a flexibility skill. In the forward walkover, the gymnast moves from a stand to a handstand, through a bridge position, and back to a stand. In the backward walkover, the gymnast lowers herself slowly backward to her hands through a bridge position, then kicks to the handstand and returns to her feet.

Whip-up

The whip-up is performed on the balance beam when the gymnast swings her legs upward and backward from a crotch support position.

INDEX